Children's Ministry Wake Up Call

Children's Ministry Wake Up Call

Preparing Ourselves to Reach Tomorrow's Generation

Esther Moreno

Foreword by Ryan Frank

ISBN:	Softcover	978-1-7960-7806-0
	eBook	978-1-7960-7813-8

This is a work of fiction. Names, characters, places and incidents either are the product of the author's imagination or are used fictitiously, and any resemblance to any actual persons, living or dead, events, or locales is entirely coincidental.

Print information available on the last page.

Rev. date: 12/12/2019

To order additional copies of this book, contact:
Xlibris
1-888-795-4274
www.Xlibris.com
Orders@Xlibris.com
807083

I dedicate this book to my dad, Rev. Dr. Michael Miller Sr., whose example made me the leader I am today.

Contents

Acknowledgements

I am so grateful for all of the amazing opportunities God has given me to expand my reach in my ministry to children. A ministry I know wouldn't be possible without the help and support of so many who have rallied around me and my vision. Together, they share in my belief that every child is a precious gift from God created for His purposes. Without them knowing it, they have joined me in this war for the next generation as we fight to reach the hearts and minds of every child with the gospel of Jesus Christ. To all those who have invited me on their platforms, who have joined me on mine, and who have invited me into their homes and churches through virtual trainings and more, Thank you!

Thank you to my brilliant husband Guylando Moreno who I sometimes confuse for Superman. He has labored alongside me in my quest to reach the next generation. His love and support have been invaluable to me. Despite his busy career, he has helped me to capture every star I've ever reached for, and for that I am eternally grateful. Also, special thanks to my wonderful in-laws, Kim Moreno-Mays and Larry Mays, for loving my children as their own through every workshop, project, and special event. They have gone above and beyond the call of duty, sometimes with extremely short notice to ensure our children are well taken care of. I certainly wouldn't be able to do all that I do without them. The day I became their daughter was a blessed day indeed.

Lastly, I would be remiss if I didn't thank my dear friend Ricardo Miller from Effective Living LLC who has been more than a friend. He has been a mentor and much needed sounding board. Thank you for seeing my passion 5 years ago and consistently investing in my growth and development. You have served to strengthen my resolve in reaching children and for that I will forever be grateful.

Foreword

I have the great privilege of interacting with leaders every day. Every once in a while, I meet someone who really captures my attention. That's what happened when I met Esther Moreno.

I described Esther as a "rising star" in the Children's Ministry community to my team and immediately reached out to her so we could build a friendship. I've grown to appreciate Esther's passion for Children's Ministry and for empowering leaders to go to the next level. As a result, I have invited Esther to join me on webinars, online trainings, and most recently on the main stage at my conference, Kidmin Nation Mega Con.

Esther knows how to think like a leader. She understands that the biggest difference between success and failure is the way you think. This is precisely why she wrote *Children's Ministry Wake Up Call.* This work serves as an undeniable reminder that our victory in the Christian life, ministry, careers, and our life's work is about the way we think. In view of this, she challenges us to elevate our ministries by examining our principles and methods. She pushes us to incorporate digital technology and creative teaching, without sacrificing the authentic connection that require a healthy ministry to thrive and flourish.

Above all, she reminds us that the sum total of our ministry to children is a byproduct of our personal walk with the Lord. It's important that every day you're taking care of yourself spiritually. It's important that every day you are taking care of yourself physically and emotionally. You need to make sure that your relationships are right because your mindset is a key to victory or defeat in life and in ministry.

This resource from Esther will help you think the way God wants you to think about Children's Ministry. It will help you overcome challenges that seem way too big. It will help you process problems that seem too difficult. It will help you identify areas where you need to grow and change. It will help you see yourself the way God sees you.

I am honored to write the foreword to *Children's Ministry Wake Up Call.* I know it will bless you beyond belief. I can't wait for you to dig in. I sure wish it had been around when I started in Children's Ministry many years ago. (I'm not telling you how many years it has been!)

Blessings to each of you!

Ryan Frank
Kidz Matter – CEO and Publisher

"We hold in our hands their destiny. We determine largely whether they fail or they succeed. What they are today, the world of tomorrow will be."

-- Ricardo Miller

Introduction

Everything is changing. For those of us who are passionate about reaching the next generation with the gospel of Jesus Christ, it is absolutely critical that we understand not only where Children's Ministry is but where it needs to go. The time for action is now. Church attendance is dropping precipitously. The suicide rate among youth is rising. Cyberbullying, sex trafficking, school shootings, and online predators are far too prevalent to be ignored. All manner of unsound doctrine and new age philosophies are enchanting the hearts and minds of our children. Their access to unprecedented information is only a click away, and their views of authority, morality, and God are under attack. In short, we are in a war for the hearts and minds of the next generation. Yet despite all of these warning signs, Children's Ministry leaders are finding it difficult to move beyond the standard approaches, which are ill-suited and ill-equipped to address the needs of this generation.

If the church wants to be here tomorrow, then we are going to have to develop a new approach that is adept and prepared to reach this generation like never before. It's going to require that we leverage the best technology because that's the world that they live in. It demands a paradigm shift in our approach authentically engaging and connecting with the children in terms they understand. The future of Children's Ministry requires that we address the "taboo" topics of the day head-on instead of tiptoeing around the uncomfortable issues. It is going to necessitate a reevaluation of our methods while preserving our principles. It will dictate a certain level of investigation, innovation, and creativity across our teaching so that it engages children of today and tomorrow. The future of Children's Ministry is going to require that our ministries become truly spirit-led instead of space or program-centered.

In short, this means that we have to move beyond the Children's Ministry 1.0 status quo. It requires that we position ourselves to become the church of tomorrow. One that considers the shifting demographics in the communities that we are called to serve. It means that leaders do the difficult work of understanding the schemes and temptations that stalk the children of this generation. We can no longer ignore this transformative digital age, but must effectively harness it for God's glory.

In my first work, *Children's Ministry Moving Forward*, I talked about the basics. In this work, I am urging Children's Ministry leaders to appreciate changing seasons and to prepare themselves for the coming war. We are called for such a time as this, and must become the church that this generation so desperately needs. It is my prayer that you will invest the time, take notes, and seriously consider the truth embedded within the pages, stories, and scriptures contained herein. Consider starting a study group with your team to discuss the topics within this book. Allow the ideas to help you become more effective in your service to children and families. Don't become outdated in your call to reach the next generation. I believe that this book is about to bless you and your department. Buckle your seatbelts because it's going to be a ride. Are you ready? Then let's begin…

1

Principles vs. Methods

"It's time to Wake Up and understand that Principles don't change, but Methods do."

Methods

Now that's a statement worth repeating: Understanding that principles don't change, methods do. If we ever hope to become effective Children's Ministry Leaders, then it is time for us to wake up and embrace this idea that **principles don't change, but methods do**. Simply stated, methods are the way we choose to do something, or our strategic spin on how we carry out a task. Every day our lives are filled with methods that help us get from one day to the next. Methods are ingrained in every pattern of our lives, ranging from how we convince our kids to eat their vegetables, to how we get that bashful child to open up and participate during Wednesday night programming. If you work with children, then you know we are forever searching to find that perfect method to reach the hearts and minds of the next generation.

Some methods are more effective than others. I will never forget the first child that was absolutely impervious to what I like to call the "Esther Joy Bomb!" Animated enthusiasm has always been my method of choice when it comes to engaging children. For years, I have seen my enthusiasm and joy excite many a child, but for this little boy it was completely different. In fact, I think it turned him off. Literally! After a series of lackluster responses from him, I convinced myself that I needed to turn up the intensity with an over-the-top, joyful, exuberant, and personalized greeting. Surely, he would be my biggest fan after such a display because no child could possibly resist the full extent of the Esther Joy Bomb. Boy did that plan backfire! I can honestly say that I have never witnessed a child jump so high until that moment. I spent months wracking my brain around what particular method I could implement to reach this special child. Well, I am happy to report that after many failed attempts, my little friend finally warmed up to me, and even gifted me with the occasional high-five. Method of choice: time, attention, and a whole lot of love. For him, I learned that I also had to tap into my quieter, less energetic side (which, if you know me was extremely difficult) but it was totally worth it. I still cherish our brief but sweet conversations that provided me with an invaluable glimpse of what was going on in his world. An honesty and visibility that would have been impossible if I were not willing to try a different approach.

There is not a one size fits all method that will work for every child. Children are different and they come into our children's ministries with different needs. We should be as sensitive to those needs as possible, and never try to squeeze them into a "generic kid" box. **If we are intentional about knowing our children, then we position ourselves to detect their needs and respond accordingly.** But knowing our children or the best method to meet their needs is not enough. We must be even more vigilant to submit our ways to God and allow him to perfect our methods.

While it's great to come alongside a strong team and debate the best methods, these strategies must nonetheless be drenched in prayer and spirit led. We must come humbly before the Father, not superficially, but as those in desperate need of His direction. Similar to the young Solomon after he was anointed king, we must approach God with complete dependency and trust. Like him, we must not only rely on our positions or natural abilities, but fully appreciate that without God's divine gift of wisdom we would be utterly incapable of fulfilling His plan for our lives. Solomon's desperation for God's ways leap off the page as you read 2 Kings 3:7- 9.

If we are truly going to impact the next generation for Christ, Children's Ministry Leaders must prioritize their personal relationships with the Lord. Spending time with God in prayer, regularly reading His Word, and seeking times of refreshing from His presence will be vital attributes in the effective Children's Ministry Leader of the future. Only then can we be sensitive to God's leadings when it comes to the particular methods he desires us to use and those we must change.

Why Should We Hold Methods Loosely

Methods have to change because people change, generations change, and circumstances change. Because our world is in a continual state of change, **it is vital that Children's Ministry leaders of tomorrow be open-minded, ready, and willing to shift their methods at any time to better reach children and families**. As leaders, we should always be in the business of assessing and taking an honest appraisal of what's working and what's not.

Changes are happening all around us every day. In my friend Tammy's case, the forecast changed. What was supposed to be a beautiful sunny day quickly turned into a dreary downpour. She woke up horrified as she had finally convinced her church to schedule their very first trunk-or-treat. As the newest member to the church staff, Tammy was very concerned about the success of this event. I still remember the phone call I received the morning of the event urging me to pray for clear skies by 5pm that evening. Well, the Lord answered our prayers with a gracious "no," as the rain continued to pour well past 5pm. My poor friend was left with two choices: to change her method or to cancel. I was happy to hear that the church decided to shift their approach and move the event indoors. The new method kept families dry, warm, happy, and numbers up for what was considered by all to be an extremely successful trunk-or-treat. From the pictures that circulated on social media, it was no question that it was fun had by all. How easy it would have been for my friend to cancel her event. To begrudgingly admit defeat and say, "well...we tried, but our original method is no longer going to work; so make it a great evening friends, and better luck next year."

How easy it is for us to quit and become discouraged when our methods and plans seem to fall short of the effectiveness we had envisioned. Maybe it's a method that had flourished for decades, but now is completely ineffective. Maybe the forecast hasn't changed, but the community has. When we aren't sensitive to the shifts that happen around us, we can find ourselves implementing outdated methods that are ineffective in reaching our ultimate goal. **As Children's Ministry leaders moving forward, we must have the courage to change methods that are no longer working.** Even more, we must have the courage to challenge outdated methods, even if those once effective methods were created by individuals that we hold in high regard. Trust me, I understand that this can be a quite uncomfortable and intimidating undertaking. For years I struggled with people pleasing, always wanting to make everyone happy. My desire to please people blinded me to dead programming, and allowed me to easily fall into the "because we've always done it this way" trap. Besides, it was special to them. I was doing a good thing, right? Even though I knew there were far superior methods available, I justified maintaining these bad ideas if it allowed me to stroke a few egos and keep the peace. This bad behavior was only compounded by the day-to-day busyness of ministry, which provided yet another excuse for failing to address the ineffective methods. But this is not the behavior of a true leader, but rather that of a children's ministry maintainer. If you've been there before, you know it's a dead place to be. I am grateful that God sent some amazing people in my life to break that destructive thinking. Real leaders aren't afraid to challenge the status quo and uproot methods that no longer work. To go back to the drawing board, though it be full, and begin to erase in an effort to draw up something bigger and better. Effective Children's Ministry Leaders Moving Forward will need to be confident in what they have to bring to the table, bold enough to challenge ineffective methods for the greater good, and brave enough to maintain a healthy sense of honor for those around them.

Perhaps there is no better illustration of this than David when he was preparing to face Goliath. We meet David as a young shepherd boy. Some might call David inexperienced, especially when it came to battle. Unsurprisingly, King Saul sought to shoehorn him into the "classic shield and armor" expected of every soldier in his army. But there was David, weighed down by someone else's armor wrapped in the tunic of the mighty king that sat before him. But David, confident in his abilities and even more confident in the God that ordered his steps, chose another way. David's method of choice: five smooth stones, a shepherd's bag, and a sling. David brought a different method to the battleground that day. While it proved to be an effective method, I'm sure that it nonetheless shocked many of his contemporaries who likely scoffed at what seemed to be a woefully deficient wardrobe to face a giant. It was an epic moment. God chose David to defeat Goliath. **He chose you too. He has gifted you with exactly what you need to be successful right where you are. He has brought you to a place for such a time, and prepared good works that only you can accomplish.** May we go forth as confident as David. Even though we may be small in men's eyes, we know within us is the power to defeat giants.

Another lesson to be gleaned from David was his ability to show honor to his predecessor. Even after rising in popularity and strength, he never hesitated to show Saul honor, whether he agreed with his methods or not. This practice continued after Saul's death. Do you show honor? It can be so easy to come into an environment and make changes right away in areas you deem to be problematic. But **the best leaders are those who are able to identify areas of improvement and make the necessary changes while showing honor to the designers of those previous methods**. The truth is, those methods at one time did work and blessed many. Good Children's Ministry leaders are sensitive to that and implement changes with the utmost grace and respect for the past and hope for the future. I have witnessed firsthand the painful consequences of implementing change with no honor. The havoc it wreaks and the backbiting it breeds can have a tendency to bring about more confusion than productive change. We should never negatively put our mouths on methods of the past only to humiliate others. Trust me, it sends a message you do not want to send. There were many a people who approached David to impress him by dishonoring Saul and were surprised with the "off with his head" verdict. Now we certainly don't want to chop off anyone's head, but we should be clear that we take no delight in corrosive speech that dishonors others. Conversely, **as new leaders come in, it is important that old leaders honor them by giving them a chance and trusting the fresh eye they bring to the ministry.**

Principles

As we have discussed, methods change and that's okay. But when it comes to principles, those should always stay the same. Principles are universal. They are eternal and they don't change. Principles are the very foundations on which we stand, and serve as the guiding light for our methods. They are the ultimate, immutable, and non-negotiable reason why we do what we do, and in their absence everything that we do is in vain. For example, I use the method of sneaking dark green leafy vegetables into my son's smoothies because of the underlying principle that the intake of nutritious foods is vital to him reaching optimal health. The same is true in our church work. Sunday after Sunday we labor through a variety of methods to create a dynamic worship experience for children and their families in pursuit of the ultimate goal of helping them to know Christ. The methods are many. From rocking babies in the nursery to leading a rambunctious group of 5th grade boys in Bible study, what keeps us going is our principles. It's the faith that motivates us to show up and roll up our sleeves because it seeks every opportunity to plant an eternal seed in the hearts and minds of little ones.

It is this principle that has often served as an anchor during the most challenging of seasons. It kept me going one evening during what I assumed was to be a normal evening of Awana. For those unfamiliar with Awana, it is a global non-profit ministry dedicated to providing

Bible-based evangelism and discipleship programming for children ages 2- 18. As co-leader for the "Awana Cubbies," otherwise known as the preschool fun bunch, it was my job to lead the cutest and most stubborn clubbers our program had to offer. Coerced to take the role by a friend, I reluctantly accepted the title and co-led with her in exchange for free dinners every Thursday night. But I stood by the underlying principle of the Awana Club and proudly recited it in their pledge with all the children every Thursday. Some of you may know it, "We are the Awana Club...whose goal is to reach boys and girls with the Gospel of Jesus Christ and train them to serve him." It was that principle that kept me showing up every Thursday evening for the next 3 years, even when I felt depleted from the happenings of the week and my own position as a Children's Pastor.

I will never forget when what was supposed to be typical Awana Thursday was completely turned upside down. It all begin when one of my junior leaders summoned me into the bathroom for what he deemed to be a 911 emergency. When I had arrived, I was directed to one of the stalls where one of our 4 year old Cubbies had developed a case of explosive diarrhea! I wish I could say that I smiled with compassion and began to glow like Moses after his encounter with God on the mountain. But that would be a bold face lie. My actual response was more along the following lines: "Oh Lord, Why me?!!!!" It was in that moment when I had to cling to my principles like never before, and remember why I was called to be there. Weak stomach and all, I wiped that poor baby's bottom knowing there was no possible way to preserve his dignity and wait for his guardian to arrive. As I made my way back to the classroom with a relieved Cubby at my side, I was met by my co- director restraining her own laughter having dodged the bathroom adventure. During parent pick-up, the boy's mother stopped me. She thanked me for cleaning up her baby. With tears in her eyes, she expressed the great love and appreciation for my willingness to care for her child in a way that went well-beyond her expectations. Never had I imagined such a task would have had such a profound effect on someone. It's funny how God uses the most mundane or messiest of situations to reveal His glory. In the midst of toilet paper, and we used a lot, was a vital lesson of servanthood for all three of us. As Christ served us and cleaned up our mess on the cross, so we do the same for others. **There is true fulfillment to be experienced even in the most insignificant of tasks, if we perform them through the conviction of our principles.**

How Are Methods & Principles Being Challenged

My husband and I have been married for a blissful 11 years now. I can recall the early years of our relationship when our metabolisms were a lot faster and the threat of male patterned baldness wasn't a concern. We would spend many a date night going to Blockbuster Video picking out our favorite new releases and cuddling up as we binged on buttered popcorn until we passed out. It was the perfect method to catch up on the newest movies. The principle was simple: provide convenient entertainment. Back then, we were more than happy to drive up to the local video store and browse the aisles for our favorite picks. But it wasn't long until a little invention called Netflix entered the scene. This new method ultimately provided access to a variety of movies and shows through streaming services from the comfort of our own home. It wasn't long before our Friday night trips to Blockbuster were completely replaced by the plethora of options we had from our couch.

We saw a similar shift in methods when Toys R Us made the decision to close their doors. My own shock at this announcement quickly subsided as I slowly realized that – in spite of my nostalgic dismay – I couldn't remember the last time I had actually gone into a toy store to purchase toys. With the development of innovative companies like Amazon, I no longer needed to walk into a brick & mortar store to purchase anything, especially toys.

So what do Blockbuster and Toys R Us have in common? Let's just say there was a cultural shift, and they definitely missed the boat. Their commitment to their principles was great, but their inability to part with outdated methods cost them everything. Unfortunately, they were no match for the innovative businesses that came in after them with the exact same principle of providing convenient entertainment and services, but operated under a more effective method, which was better suited to the preferences of a changing world.

As Children's Ministry leaders, it is vital that we wake up and become cognizant of the changes and cultural shifts that are happening in our communities, schools, and beyond. **It is vital that we constantly evaluate, assess, and tweak those things that are not producing the desired outcome, and create innovative ideas that are relevant to the community around us**. To separate innovative thinking from the way we "do" church is a grave mistake and will cost us greatly. Do you know the demographics of the surrounding community in which your ministry is planted? Are the methods you're using to reach the children and their families built around the modern family of today or that of yesterday?

So here's your homework assignment. Look at the warning signs below. Evaluate your current methods for reaching children and their families. Take an honest unbiased look at the way you do things. The proof is in the pudding! Get your Children's Ministry team together and if you don't have a team yet, get busy! Strong Children's Ministries are built upon even stronger teams, so if you don't have one, you've got yourself a problem! We will discuss that more in Chapter 6. Do your methods fit into any of these categories? If yes, let's have the courage to shift the way we do things so that we can reach the next generation for Christ and truly become the kingdom builders we were created to be.

- The Young people are saying it's outdated. People in general are saying it's outdated. When the world is screaming at you, do it and God a favor, LISTEN!
- It's Outdated! Just in case you didn't hear me the first time. I don't think I can emphasize this enough! We have got to stop forcing the next generation into the box of the old! There is a new generation out there that can be reached if we are willing to get outside of the box and reach them!
- Something has shown itself to be a better method than previous ones used. If it's better, it's better! Stop over analyzing and

produce! And when something comes along even better than that be willing to shift!

- The method is liked but is not producing the same results it once did. Honor the ways of the past and move on if you want to exist in the future!
- It is evident that the spirit of denial has captured the hearts of particular people and it's killing the work. When people are in denial they will justify their position to the death! These people are always making excuses for why things are not working, namely blaming others around them, rather than assuming responsibility for an ineffective method. If you don't address this head on your church will suffer gravely! Confront in grace and commit to moving forward!!!

Do you hear an alarm? IT'S TIME TO WAKE UP!

Key Points

- Children's Ministries moving forward must embrace the fact that Principles don't change, but Methods do!
- If we are intentional about knowing our children, then we position ourselves to detect their needs and respond accordingly.
- If we are truly going to impact the next generation for Christ, Children's Ministry Leaders must prioritize their personal relationships with the Lord.
- It is vital that Children's Ministry leaders of tomorrow be open-minded, ready, and willing to shift their methods at any time to better reach children and families.
- As Children's Ministry leaders, we must have the courage to change methods that are no longer working.
- God chose you! He has gifted you with exactly what you need to be successful right where you are. He has brought you to a place for such a time, and prepared good works that only you can accomplish.
- The best leaders are those who are able to identify areas of improvement and make the necessary changes while showing honor to the designers of those previous methods.
- As new leaders come in, it is important that old leaders honor them by giving them a chance and trusting the fresh eye they bring to the ministry.
- There is true fulfillment to be experienced even in the most insignificant of tasks, if we perform them through the conviction of our principles.
- It is vital that we constantly evaluate, assess, and tweak those things that are not producing the desired outcome, and create innovative ideas that are relevant to the community around us.

2

Digital Technology

"The Rooster just crowed, it's time to go digital or go home!"

Neither do people pour new wine into old wineskins. If they do, the skins will burst; the wine will run out and the wineskins will be ruined. No, they pour new wine into new wineskins, and both are preserved. Matthew 9:17

Everything's Changing

Last year, I was so excited for Christmas because my son was finally old enough to embrace the magic of the season. Having attained the ripe age of 4, surely this would be the year that he would take more joy in his actual toys, rather than their packaging. This would be the year that his little heart would experience true excitement over the secret packages that lay under the tree. In preparation, I had spent months shopping for the top toys for his age group that he was sure to flip over. On Christmas Eve, I spent hours wrapping presents throughout the night. My eagerness to see my son's Christmas joy carefully counterbalanced my exhaust-induced zombie demeanor. Honestly, it made me reminisce on my own childhood and the joy my siblings and I experienced tearing into our gifts at his age and beyond. We would spend untold hours playing with our new toys for well into the night. When the faithful morning had come, my son had expressed joy for sure. But within an hour of unwrapping gifts, it wasn't long until he was badgering us to see our mobile devices so he could play his favorite games. I immediately thought to myself, what's wrong with this kid! You have a trove of new treasures before you and you prefer to play with gaming apps on our cellphones! Little did I know that it was me who had lost touch with reality.

If there's one thing that's for sure, it's that everything is changing. Now that's a fact you can count on! And if we ever hope to reach the next generation for Christ, then we need to be open minded to the idea that we may have to reevaluate the way we do things. This is non-negotiable if the message we carry is going to remain relevant to young people. One of the most pivotal changes experienced in the past century is this monumental, cataclysmic, paradigm shift into what is commonly known as the digital age. The digital age is here and it's transforming the way we do everything, including how we read the Bible, watch TV, and listen to music. The reach of this digital transformation has affected how we shop, how kids are learning in school, how we interact with people, and the list goes on. **Our children are not growing up in the same world that we did. With the perpetual and rapid development of innovative technology, our children are able to do things more efficiently, faster, and go further.** And while these rapid technological leaps may be intimidating to some, this is their world and they are entirely comfortable with it. The quicker we can embrace this truth, the faster we can effectively minister to this generation.

So how open are you to change? The truth is, the older we get, the harder it is to change. Don't be too hard on yourself if this is an area of struggle for you. I still struggle with the temptation to have those late night snacks because it was something I did for years. Unfortunately, the failure to embrace technology may have much more devastating consequences than a few midnight calories. **Our inability to communicate with them in their own language and context may leave us with a generation unresponsive and resistant to the message of hope.**

When we force the next generation into the box of "how we learned it," we fall into what I like to call the "new wine in old wineskins" trap. Jesus warned us what happens when we make this mistake: it bursts! The same thing happens when we force our old ways onto the young instead of reaching them in a way that they can relate to. Holding too tight to our traditions can result in our ministry to children bursting and our messages falling flat. Even worse, the Word of God may be seen as stodgy, irrelevant, and boring. It's only when we are willing to shift our approach to better connect with a newer generation that both are preserved.

Our desire to cling to our preferred "wineskins" manifests itself in various ways, both subtle and significant. I will never forget being invited to a children's ministry service in Michigan some time ago. There was a point during the service where the children had the opportunity to earn a reward for having brought their Bibles with them. Interestingly, the value given for paperback Bibles was higher than the digital ones. To say this bothered me would an understatement. Now don't get me wrong, I love my paperback Bible. But if the church ever hopes to be ready for tomorrow, we must be able to see past our personal preferences to those of the next generation we are serving.

For children growing up in a digital age, it's only a matter of time before everything they do – including reading God's Word – moves onto a digital platform. Every Sunday more and more people are reaching for their digital devices when the pastor tells them to turn to a passage in the Bible. This change isn't coming, it's already here! How comfortable are you with this shift? At the end of the day, if a child is brought to saving faith in Christ through a digital Bible truth instead of a paperback, then would their salvation be any less valid? Of course not! The truth is the truth and holds just as much power regardless of its format. How receptive is your church to the use of digital devices for the purpose of service? Admittedly, it is not always an easy transition because of our personal experience and attachment to how effective it was for us. But the transition becomes a bit smoother if we begin to appreciate the potential that new ways to approach God and his Word can bring. Imagine it. With the aid of technology, our grandchildren may understand the Bible with a speed and depth that we can't imagine. Just like lexicons, concordances, and other devotional studies made God's word accessible to countless people, the tools of tomorrow may open untold Biblical treasures, cross-references, and multiple translations at the swipe of a finger. Remember methods are adaptable, provided the truth remains eternal.

Is your temperament toward digital technology one that supports the generation you are ministering to, or one that makes them want to run for the hills? If your answer to these questions aren't ones to be desired, know that there's hope! It's never too late to connect with these digital natives as we become intentional in researching and understanding our audience.

Digital Natives, the New Audience

You recognize them, and if you're in Children's Ministry, you love them. They are the little people that fill up your Children's Church, classrooms, and midweek programs. They are the junior leaders that help assist in a variety of ways in your Children's Ministry department. They are Generation Z! Do you know them? They are extremely educated. They are the most ethnically diverse generation yet, and the most tech savvy generation known to man. So let me ask you again. Do you know them? Do you know this audience of digital natives? I hope you do because their eyes are on you, watching to see what this Christ thing is all about. Are you ready to spread the message of hope to them in engaging ways that capture their attention?

Now is the time for Children's Ministry leaders to rise up and stop making excuses for the disconnect between generations because of their failure to understand these digital natives. Children's Ministry leaders of tomorrow must be committed to investing time to understand the generation that populate their ministries. At the end of the day, these children are growing up in a digital age and if you truly want to reach them, then you better learn how to plug-in and get connected. Doing things the way they've always been done will no longer be acceptable.

The reality is, if you're not willing to put in the work to learn the language of the digital age, then it may be time for you to retire from Children's Ministry. We have to make room for those more willing to passionately pursue the next generation and put forth the effort required to reach them for Christ.

Similar to learning any new language, there will be great challenges, but it is a worthy sacrifice. I will not soon forget the many opportunities my husband and I have been given to travel to the Yucatan region of Mexico to minister in a village there called Xochempich. For three consecutive years, we looked forward to traveling to this small town to do mission work and connect with families there. Anyone who knows my husband knows that he is very proficient in Spanish. A skill that I definitely do not possess. I can remember the children running up to him in the village. They loved him! As a children's pastor, I can recall a moment of jealousy that I had experienced. I was constantly in awe of how easy it was for him to connect with them as I struggled to belt out the simplest of Spanish phrases. I would never disregard the work that God did in and through me those 3 years, language barriers and all. But, I will say that I was hindered in my reach in ways my husband was not because he knew the language. The same is true for us when we neglect learning the language of the digital natives that consume our ministries. **While our superficial knowledge may help us get by, this knowledge gap significantly undermines our ability to connect with them and hinders the effectiveness of our message.**

If there is anyone who knew the importance of understanding the language of those around him, it was definitely the Apostle Paul. Paul was multilingual and knew a variety of languages including Greek, Aramaic, Hebrew, and possibly some Latin. Beyond that, Paul was a master at understanding his audience. He studied the times and made real investments to know people and their cultural context. He became a student of world views and made it his business to be culturally aware. In fact, it was that very knowledge of the culture that he leveraged as reference points to grab the attention of his audience and reach them more effectively for Christ; and why? Paul makes his reasoning clear in 1 Corinthians chapter 9:

"I have become all things to all people so that by all possible means I might save some. I do this all for the sake of the gospel, that I may share in it's blessings." Matthew 9:22

Does your approach mirror Paul's when it comes to reaching the children in your ministry? Can you honestly say that you've put in the work to learn their digital language? Have you studied the times of the next generation that lay before you? Have you done your homework; are you up to date on what's trending with the young people you serve? Have you researched the games they play, the music they love, or the social media apps they use? Do you use that knowledge of their culture as a reference point to draw them in to the message of hope? Above all, Jesus has called us to be fishers of men. They may have been fishing in regular waters, but we are wading into digital waves. They may have casted fishing nets, but we're dealing with the internet. They may have used a traditional hook, while ours is a digital hook. But the objective remains the same, we are called to be witnesses to the gospel of Jesus Christ and fulfill the great commission. Have you equipped yourself with the appropriate tools to catch the little fish in your waters?

Leveraging Tech in Your Kidmin Department

When it comes to incorporating digital technology into your Kidmin department, we have to remember that technology is created to help us work smarter and not harder! It is essential that we get to work and ASSESS, ASSESS, ASSESS!

1. Assess the needs of your particular department
2. Assess where changes need to be made
3. Assess the budget

When it comes to assessing the needs of your particular department, consider the needs that are unique to your church as a whole. Where can digital technology really help your ministry? For example, if the rooms you use for children are tech free, then maybe you need a screen installed to better connect with the digital natives in your ministry. If you're still checking in kids by hand, then consider installing secure check-in stations. **Successful Children's Ministry departments of tomorrow will take advantage of the efficiency that digital technology provides and intersperse it throughout as needed, both administratively and in their weekly programming**.

The churches who refuse to adapt and are adamant about keeping things the way they've always been will lose. The churches who are still functioning off of felt boards, VHS cassette tapes, and manual sign-in sheets will turn into the churches of yesterday. As Children's Ministry Leaders moving forward, we must honestly assess the effectiveness of our ministries and make the necessary adjustments. Without disrespecting the past, we must soberly evaluate the status quo, and be bold enough to make those future changes required to reach the next generation.

While evaluating the needs of our ministries, we must also assess our budget so that we can position ourselves to make the best decisions with the resources that have been entrusted to us. Incorporating digital technology may prove to be a bigger undertaking for some than for others. **Remember, it's okay to take baby steps on your digital journey. Some projects can be completed today, and others will have to wait for tomorrow. It's okay! Honor your budget, set a plan, and you will get there.**

Need a little more direction? Consider the following when looking for ways to incorporate digital technology in your children's ministry:

- Use Visuals & Digital Presentations: This is especially important when engaging children because it invites them to use their imaginations. Use popular movies that are trending to show clips, and inspire themes for your environments. There are a variety of digital clips that come with many curriculums on the market. Don't have one? Find some online or make your own. YouTube is a great place to start. Remember, [successful children's ministries of tomorrow] will be equipped with the necessary audio visual equipment to meet the needs of the digital natives they serve. If you don't have it, that's your first assignment.

- Consider Convenience Apps & Devices: I always recommend having a bluetooth speaker on hand in the event of an emergency. Also, remote control devices can serve as lifesavers if you're low on help in the media department. Being able to flip slides with the click of a button or swipe of a finger can minimize stress and keep the show running smoothly without distractions.
- Use Planning & Organizational Tools: Many churches are already utilizing church management software for the purposes of attendance tracking, child check- in, event management, member directories, member portals, multi-site management, online giving, volunteer management, and more. Are you one of them? Other tools like dropbox and google docs offer a wealth of assistance when it comes to organization in your Kidmin. If you don't know what they are and how you can use them, it's time to do your homework! Smart devices like Alexa, Echo, and Google Assistant also help to provide immediate assistance right when we need them.
- Embrace New Ways of Communication: If you are not utilizing social media, you are limiting your reach big time! If the best way to reach millennials is through social media outlets, how much more Generation Z and beyond? If we continue to insist on using the same old methods of communication to get our messages out, they will continue to fall flat. Consider using resources like zoom for live webinars or free conference calls to have meetings with your team from the comfort of your own home. The goal is to get your message heard. So if you are uncomfortable with digital forms of communication, it's time to get over yourself and get plugged in!

Bridging the Gap Between Parents & the Digital Age

With the rapid advancements of technology, it's becoming harder and harder for parents to keep up with all the changes that are constantly happening in the world of their digital natives. Digital technology can be a very scary and intimidating world for parents. The truth is that kid's addiction to digital technology is real, cyberbullying is real, and online predators are real. **As Children's Ministry leaders, we can never replaces parents, but we can come alongside and equip them with effective tools and resources to help them navigate this digital age with confidence**. At the end of the day, the digital age is here and it's not going anywhere. Helping parents to embrace that truth while encouraging them to be watchmen and mentors when it comes to their child's digital use is vital. Remember, we have to be just as informed in order to inform. These days, as incredible as technology can be, with all of the underlying dangers, parents can't afford to turn a blind eye to their child's digital usage. Here are some tips to help the parents in your ministry stay ahead of the digital game:

- Encourage Parents Not to Shun Technology: Encourage parents to not avoid technology as intimidating as it may be. Rather, encourage them to become intentional about learning about the apps that are of most interest to their kids. Staying up to date is key! Remember, too much of anything can be bad, but avoidance is just as bad.
- Be Aware: Encourage parents to be aware on all fronts. Be aware of why their kids like what they like, but also be sensitive to the dangers that may accompany their preferences. Commonsensemedia.org is a great resource for parents and Children's Ministry leaders alike to check reviews on popular movies, gaming, and social media apps.
- Provide Resources: Provide applicable trainings, books, and monthly updates on changes in the digital world for kids to help better equip the parents in your ministry.

- Go Digital: Encourage parents to leverage technology in positive ways. For example, text 5 things you love about your daughter, pray in FaceTime with your children, challenge your child to a competition on their favorite app. Empower parents to retire old methods and to incorporate things like Alexa, Siri, Smart phones, and Bible Apps.

The Rooster has crowed. It's time to WAKE UP and go digital!

Key Points

- ❖ If there's one thing that's for sure, it's that everything is changing!
- ❖ He chose you too. He has gifted you with exactly what you need to be successful right where you are. He has brought you to a place for such a time, and prepared good works that only you can accomplish.
- ❖ Our inability to communicate with children in their own language and context may leave us with a generation unresponsive and resistant to the message of hope.
- ❖ While our superficial knowledge may help us get by, knowledge gaps significantly undermine our ability to connect with children and hinders the effectiveness of our message.
- ❖ For children growing up in a digital age, it's only a matter of time before everything they do – including reading God's Word – moves onto a digital platform.
- ❖ The reality is, if you're not willing to put in the work to learn the language of the digital age, then it may be time for you to retire from Children's Ministry.
- ❖ Successful Children's Ministry departments of tomorrow will take advantage of the efficiency that digital technology provides and intersperse it throughout as needed, both administratively and in their weekly programming.
- ❖ Remember, it's okay to take baby steps on your digital journey. Some projects can be completed today, and others will have to wait for tomorrow. It's okay! Honor your budget, set a plan, and you will get there.
- ❖ The churches who refuse to adapt and are adamant about keeping things the way they've always been will lose.
- ❖ As Children's Ministry leaders, we can never replace parents, but we can come alongside and equip them with effective tools and resources to help them navigate this digital age with confidence.

3

Creative Teaching

"It's time to go to bed early so you can Wake Up on time and prepare! Preparation is critical for this generation."

"Prepare your work outside; get everything ready for yourself in the field, and after that build your house." -Proverbs 24:27

Are You Ready?

The day of winging it is over. In a world where kids have access to all matter of information at their fingertips, they are no longer going to accept what you say just because you said it. Children's Ministry Leaders moving forward will utilize creative teaching to capture the hearts and minds of the children they serve. Such a feat is impossible without appropriate preparation. If you haven't heard this yet, it's definitely a saying worth remembering: If you fail to plan, you plan to fail. **Proper preparation can be the difference between effective and ineffective ministries.** The consequence of which can be the difference between life and death, maturity and immaturity, and winning and losing the hearts and minds of an entire generation. Those Children's Ministries whose workers wait until the last minute to look at their lessons will lose. It is vital that leaders stop making excuses and begin to give their lessons the appropriate amount of pre-planning time they deserve. Besides, kids can see right through a poorly planned lesson and when they see it, you've lost them before you've even gotten started. We can no longer afford to risk the message of truth falling flat because of pure laziness or an inability to prioritize appropriate time in the week for planning. When it comes to leading children, we must come with a spirit of excellence. Anything less will be unacceptable in the Children's Ministries of tomorrow. Warm bodies filling slots will be a thing of the past and any church left operating under such a distorted way will cause their church to die.

Our kids have a lot of questions. In a world that gives them innumerable half-truths and then says "pick one," we must ready ourselves with a spirit of excellence to provide them with the ultimate truth found only in Christ Jesus. One of the toughest questions I'd received was from an older elementary age student during vacation bible school one year. After rotating into my station, I noticed her hand up at the midway point. I assumed she had a question regarding one of the particular motions because I had led the music station that year. I was embarrassed how woefully unprepared I was to respond to her actual question. With a single inquiry, she was able to surprise me and four of my co-leaders, "Is there really only one way to get to heaven?" She went on to share a story about her good friend at school who had apparently had a different faith. "So is God not going to let her into heaven because she doesn't believe in this Christ?" We were dumbfounded and gazed at one another as to silently scream, "NOT IT!" It's not exactly a question you anticipate during a 20-minute music station where you are instructing the students on the finer points of the "flossing" dance. That day was a reminder that our children are facing challenges with their faith right now. Moving forward we must always be prepared for the tough questions our children have about the world they live in, and ready to help navigate them to the correct answers.

Changing Teaching Styles

In education utilizing multiple teaching styles is essential for helping children grasp a proper understanding of complex subject matter. With the advancements of modern technology, teaching styles are constantly changing and the church needs to pay attention! **As generations change and the way we do things evolves, it is becoming even more important that we keep up with the advancements of new teaching styles so that we can convey the foundations of the faith to our children in a way that they can understand**. When it comes to Children's Ministry, the teaching methods of yesterday are just not

going to work. You know them. Most of us grew up with them and they were just fine to us. Plus, those fish crackers during Sunday school class always sweetened the deal, regardless of the teacher's delivery. But today, we are dealing with a completely different generation. As discussed in the previous chapter, we are dealing with a generation of digital natives. In this digitally saturated world, digital learners are going to need some type of screen if we hope to retain their attention.

Bland children's ministry spaces will be a quick way to keep your numbers down! Staging and interchangeable sets designed to engage the imagination will be a must for any thriving Children's Ministry. One of the biggest misperceptions for churches who are not doing this already is that such a task is only reserved for bigger churches with a much larger budget. This couldn't be any further from the truth. I have many ministry friends from smaller churches who would agree that when it comes to creating sets, the Dollar Store is your friend! Plus, when we prepare ahead of time, we are able to jump on sales for items we would have otherwise passed up because we have a clearer picture of where we're going. By the way, it may be a good idea to plan out your series/curriculum annually. That way, you can stay on top of the things you could use all year long like that old VBS backdrop or props from another event. When it comes to creating a set, there's no deal sweeter than free!

Once you've created a killer set on a shoe-string budget, do me a favor, GET OFF OF IT! Staying on the stage is a thing of the past.

It's time to move from the stage and get among them. Sure, it may initially come across as chaotic, but it's 100x more engaging. I cannot over-emphasize proper preparation. When we come in extremely knowledgeable of our lessons, it makes it that much easier to move around and set those feet on cruise control. Even more, it gives room for the Holy Spirit to mix things up if need be without missing a beat. When I am leading a lesson, I love nothing more than to walk up and down the aisles. It gives me an opportunity to get on their level and make eye contact. In the event that you have some disrupters, you are only a few steps away from the "glance" that quickly silences all of the side conversations.

But if you're doing your job by preparing in advance, then those side conversations should be at a minimum, if at all. Let's be honest, you're always going to have a few chatterboxes. After all, this is Kidmin. But if you are keeping most of the kids' attention, you're doing an excellent job. However, if you notice a little more chatter than usual, then this can be a red flag. First, RELAX! I have seen more than one children's ministry leader crack under pressure because they couldn't keep the kids' attention. Forcing the kids into submission by throwing empty threats only goes so far. Let me tell you, if you are forcing them, then you have already lost them. There's nothing that kills a creative lesson more than the leader stopping multiple times to discipline talkers. I love talkers! They are like secret buzzards that alarm us when our lesson may not be up to par. Don't take it personally, just stop and ask yourself some questions. Why am I losing them? What could I have done differently to make this lesson more engaging? What can I do now to reel them back in? Remember, when you are preparing lessons you want them to be engaging enough to keep the kids on the edge of their seats wanting more. **Creative lessons are not one man shows or dramatic monologues. They are punctuated with drama, skits, and digital presentations.** Don't lean too much on one or you may risk losing some of your audience. Creative lessons that are sure to please are lessons created to reach every learning style.

Learning Styles

When it comes to teaching children, there are generally three main learning styles: Kinesthetic, Auditory, and Visual. **Effective Children's Ministry leaders moving forward will need to master teaching techniques that are created to reach every learning style**. Failure to do so may leave the children in your ministry feeling left behind, bored, or completely uninspired.

Kinesthetic Learners

Kinesthetic learners are those kids who shoot their hands up right away when you say, " Can I have a volunteer?" They love being active, moving around, and will take any opportunity to do so. These are your movers and shakers. Often referred to as the "bad kids" but don't make that mistake! They like to touch things in order to learn about them and have a preference for more experiential learning opportunities, so don't disappoint. Remember, kinesthetic learners love to move, so high energy worship will always help fit the bill. Also, when you are teaching a lesson and you need help from the audience, try to consider calling on those kids who you can discern are busting at the seams to get up and move. If you want to bring the Word of God to life for these learners, anything that involves physical activity is a must. Make sure you are providing enough variety in your lesson so that they're not being forced to sit in one spot for extended amounts of time.

Auditory Learners

You can think of these types of learners as the classic old school teacher's pet. Auditory learners are the kids that likely benefit from traditional methods of teaching. These learners are often assumed to be "the good kids" because they're the ones that seem to be really engaged, listening intently to your message. Since their learning is tied more to their sense of hearing, they tend to get more out of a lecturing style of teaching, provided it is supplemented with a little gusto and vocal inflections to maintain interest. They are still children after all. These children prefer to read out loud rather than silently to themselves. Auditory learners also retain information well through creative word patterns and love music. Try to turn the memory verse into fun songs and really get these children's engagement wheels turning!

Visual Learners

You've heard the saying that a picture is worth a thousand words. Well, for visual learners, a picture is probably worth twice that! Visual learners learn best when lessons are creatively illustrated. These learners probably constitute a large majority of the children that you minister to throughout the week. Visual learners prefer to see lessons demonstrated because for these learners seeing is believing! Visual learners won't grasp a message simply because you are telling it to them like auditory learners. In order to make a message stick for this creative bunch, you must activate their sense of sight through engaging visuals. This is why creative environments are so important. The next time you are preparing a lesson, consider props laying around the house that you could use to really make your message pop.

Dealing with Attention Deficit Disorder

It's an uncomfortable topic for many parents and teachers alike. Nevertheless, Children's Ministry Leaders moving forward **will be well-equipped to face Attention Deficit Disorder head on. If our goal is to truly reach the heart of every child, then we won't allow this diagnosis to deny any child of the opportunity to meet Christ.** Time and time again, I have seen beautiful and gifted children created in the image of God labeled as the "bad kids" by short-sighted children's ministry workers. Too many well-meaning children's ministry workers have given into their frustration simply because they had no knowledge on how to handle a child living with this disorder. Toward this end, many parents fear being transparent about their child's struggles because they don't want their child to be treated differently. In some cases, these well-meaning parents leave feeling just as judged and labeled as their children. Unfortunately, many ministries are failing in this area. While they may have the heart to do right by these children and their parents, the way they go about handling them leaves much to be desired. As a result, many families dealing with this disorder in their homes choose to stay home on Sundays rather than being painfully reminded that their child is a problem by yet another children's ministry worker.

Attention Deficit Disorder has multiple symptoms, including children that are: hyperactive, easily distracted, have a hard time focusing, fidgety, impulsive, and the list goes on. Wow, I think I just named the behavior of almost every child in this digital age. And that's why it can be hard to identify, but a likely candidate to label. Some children may struggle with this disorder, but show no signs of hyperactivity leaving them just as left behind as those who do. It is unfair to the parents who entrust their children into our care, the children themselves, and the children's ministry to throw teachers blindly into classrooms without proper training. I've seen one too many gifted Children's Ministry leaders walk away from serving because of the lack of proper training. **It is vital moving forward that proper training be provided to Children's Ministry workers on effective practices when it comes to nurturing and reaching children with ADD/ADHD.** Creative lessons in the future must be designed with these kids in mind. Gone are the days of hoping "little Johnny will be 'good' today." We have to stop winging it and get serious about reaching children from all walks of life. Effective Children's Ministries in the future will come alongside these parents. They will invite ADD/ADHD professionals into the church to evaluate their spaces and ensure that their environments are welcoming to all children. **Special needs rooms with trained leaders will no longer be optional. If you don't have them, you are going to lose families.** Are the Children's Ministry workers in your church trained to nurture children with ADD/ADHD. Most churches have some type of introductory training when people sign up to serve in their children's ministries with general policies and procedures. As a first step, consider adding an extra page on how to care for children struggling with this disorder. Here are a few tips to help get you started:

- **Keep your cool:** Understand that most often a child with ADD/ADHD is not trying to outright challenge you. Often times, they are just being themselves. Be patient and keep your cool. Making a spectacle of the child in front of others or using aggressive discipline techniques only makes things worse! Christ should always be our example. Like Jesus, we must be motivated by love when dealing with any child.
- **Routine, Routine, Routine:** When it comes to dealing with children with ADD/ADHD, structure is your friend! Routines make them feel safe. Create a structure that the child can rely on and try to limit sporadic activities. That means any leader coming in winging it has got to go! No excuses. BE PREPARED!
- **Avoid activities that require sitting for extended amounts of time:** For children with ADD/ADHD, actually scratch that, for most children, moving is a part of who they are. Make sure your lesson is sensitive to that and has enough variety to peak their curiosity and keep them engaged.
- **Celebrate their effort:** My husband loves to put the dishes in the dishwasher but somehow never gets around to actually hitting the start button. He may have not accomplished the complete task but still appreciates a little acknowledgement for his efforts. So take a tip from my hubby. For children with ADD/ADHD, they may struggle finishing the tasks that you give them. Celebrate them anyway for a job well-attempted rather than a job well-done. Give as little attention to the bad as possible. It should be our goal to make every child who comes through our doors feel like a million bucks! So celebrate, celebrate, celebrate!
- **Build on their interest:** Observe the things that they enjoy. When you're creating a lesson, try to incorporate the things that you know brings them the most enjoyment. For instance, if a child really enjoys playdough, then try to incorporate an activity in the lesson where they have to create something using playdough. It's as simple as that. If you have a set curriculum,

don't be afraid to modify it. It's a great way to keep the child engaged while enhancing the effectiveness of your message. Remember, your job is to relay the gospel message of hope to children in such a way that it is received. Playing off of their interest is a great way to do that.

Up and Coming Creative Teaching Methods

As Children's Ministry Leaders, we should always be keeping an eye out for emerging methods of teaching. Staying current on effective teaching methods being used in your local school district is a great way to stay ahead of the game. Too often, the church is lagging behind when it comes to effective teaching methods. The next time your team is brainstorming on ways to creatively reach the children in your ministry, go ahead and invite some school teachers to be a part of the conversation. Just recently, I was in awe of how quickly my 8 year old daughter had retained her spelling words for the week. Some of those words would have even been difficult for adults to spell. Every week we would do repetition drills in an effort to get her ready for her spelling quiz. One day after school I had her get her pencil and paper out to write her words 4x each. When she challenged me and said she already knew them, like any good mother would do, I told her to prove it. And boy did she ever. When I inquired how she learned them so fast, she shared with me a game the teacher had created to help her learn her words at a record pace. I enjoyed watching her defeat villains until she had collected every letter she needed to spell each word. This creative teaching method, known as "Gamification," is where children learn through digital play. It allows teachers to create their own competitive games to better engage their students while simultaneously motivating them to learn.

It is unwise to turn a blind eye to the creative teaching methods in our schools. Today's kids, despite attempts to limit their digital intake by parents, are already streaming extensively throughout the day through smart boards before they even get home. Even children as young as 7 years old are being sent home with digital devices for extended learning. Teachers are using apps to help keep up with children's progress and communicate more effectively with parents. What does this tell you? If we are using old methods to reach children in our children's ministries, is it any wonder why we are struggling to keep their attention?

Jesus' Way of Communication

When it comes to creative teaching methods, may we always follow the lead of the most creative teacher who ever walked the earth. **Jesus' way of communication will forever be applicable to how we reach children**. His example is punctuated with timeless wisdom. The way we embody his approach may take various forms but the principle remains the same. Instead of sandals we may be wearing a pair of Vans or Jordans, but we come in the same spirit. Being quick to listen to the needs of our children, but remaining slow to speak and slower still to get angry because children are precious in the Father's sight. Jesus was a walking example of faith and prayed for their healing. This Christ-likeness is a central tenant of my friend Tracey's ministry. A dynamic Kidmin leader known to stop during a preschool bathroom break to pray for a child who mentions even the hint of a belly ache. Jesus spent time with people and dined with the lowly. His sermons were not lengthy but they spoke a message of acceptance that sparked trust, hope, and ultimately brought about salvation to those who were under his voice. May we follow his example as we continue to reach future generations. If we are truly going to be effective communicators moving forward, it is vital that we Wake Up and get creative in the methods we use to teach children.

Key Points

- The day of winging it is over!
- Proper preparation can be the difference between effective and ineffective ministries.
- Our kids have a lot of questions. In a world that gives them innumerable half-truths and then says "pick one," we must ready ourselves with a spirit of excellence to provide them with the ultimate truth found only in Christ Jesus.
- As generations change and the way we do things evolve, it is becoming even more important that we keep up with the advancements of new teaching styles so that we can convey the foundations of the faith to our children in a way that they can understand.
- Bland children's ministry spaces will be a quick way to keep your numbers down! Staging and interchangeable sets designed to engage the imagination will be a must for any thriving Children's Ministry.
- Effective Children's Ministry leaders moving forward will need to master teaching techniques that are created to reach every learning style.
- Creative lessons are not one man shows or dramatic monologues. They are punctuated with drama, skits, and digital presentations.
- It is vital moving forward that proper training be provided to Children's Ministry workers on effective practices when it comes to nurturing and reaching children with ADD/ADHD. If our goal is to truly reach the heart of every child, then we won't allow this diagnosis to deny any child of the opportunity to meet Christ.
- It is unwise to turn a blind eye to the creative teaching methods in our schools.
- Jesus' way of communication will forever be applicable to how we reach children.

4

More about the Heart than the Space

"People Don't Care About How Much You Know Until They Know About How Much You Care." -John Maxwell

...So do Children! Stop hitting the snooze button on matters of the heart.

"But the Lord said to Samuel, "Do not look on his appearance or on the height of his stature, because I have rejected him. For the Lord sees not as man sees: man looks on the outward appearance, but the Lord looks on the heart." -1 Samuel 16:7

Crisis in the Home

I want to tell you about a little boy named John. John attended Children's Church. Despite being in service every week, he was not engaged. He was rarely interested in the lesson and garnered the reputation of being one of the "problem children." Week in and week out, month in and month out, John was a problem. The Children's Ministry workers would regularly talk to John's mother about his behavior almost every weekend. One Wednesday evening, I took the opportunity to speak with John's mother. I shared with her that even though John may have earned himself an award for highest attendance, he was not present. But instead of ending the conversation there, we collectively brainstormed about how we could help John as we both agreed that he was heading down the wrong path.

Some time had passed and we all continued to pray for John. One of the days at pick up John's mother came in. She was obviously distraught as evidenced by the tears in her eyes. I took her off to the side and began to encourage her the best way I knew how. Just two ladies letting our hair down. Our brief conversation ended with laughs and hugs. I remember John trying his hardest to avoid all eye contact with me or his mother. Peering randomly in every other direction as to not be a distraction to the encouragement he knew his mother so desperately needed. But something different happened that day. John was smiling. John rarely expressed emotion when he was in Children's Church, but that day he did. It was a new emotion that we had never seen before. John was smiling because he saw me hug his mother. What I didn't realize is that John's mother was being abused at home and all John saw as a little boy was anger, disgust, and pain in his home environment. His father was a belligerent drunk who never showed up at church but was always ready to abuse both John and his mother when they returned.

John had not seen his mother smile in a long time, but that day something changed. John came back to Children's Church a different little boy. He began to engage more and more. I am here to tell you that this boy changed for the better. His incredible transformation was not a result of my superior teaching skills, stage props, or level of preparation, but because of the love and care we showed not only to John but to his mother.

John Maxwell is credited with saying that "people don't care how much you know until they know how much you care." This little boy is a prime example that all the emphasis we place on creating a great experience amounts to nothing if there is no heart behind ministry. Now don't get me wrong, I'm glad that you are prepared. I'm glad the environment shows creativity. I'm glad that the ministry has sufficient workers. I'm glad you're giving out snacks. I'm glad the gift shop is solid. I'm glad all the leaders are wearing matching shirts, name badges, and bright smiles. I'm glad that all of the volunteers are happy because the pastor approved for all of them to receive a $5 dollar gift card to Starbucks. But, **when you're teaching those kids, if they don't feel the connection of your heart in the ministry you're providing, then you're simply doing a production and a production doesn't change lives. Ministry does.**

A Call to Connect and Not Just Inform

As Children's Ministers, we get so excited about starting new curriculum, stocking the supply closet, and kicking off new series that we often overlook people like John and his mother. It is imperative that we intensify our efforts on connecting. **In order to connect, we must get our ministry to a place where we know who we are ministering to.** Our friend John was already labeled a troublesome kid well on the way to a horrible future. But so many of us couldn't see his behavior as the cry for help that it was. So many children in our ministries are crying out for love. They are crying out for attention. They want you to see them. They want you to understand that there may be more going on with them than meets the eye. The problem is that people can be in the same room without connecting.

This phenomenon extends beyond Children's Ministry. We live in communities where knowing your next door neighbors is becoming increasingly rare. Despite the increasing number of students in our schools, there are kids that don't have any friends. Our church numbers are continuing to increase, but service times are being cut to accommodate heavy production and programs. With all of the attention on the lights, camera, and action, it is all too easy to forget those matters of the heart. As a result, we end up not connecting at the place where real change occurs.

When I took the time to hug John's mom and see how she was doing, it spoke a message to John that was louder than any colorful stage. It told him that we were more than the program. **Effective Children's Ministry leaders moving forward must show that they are about more than just a service, but rather about the people in**

the service. Do the kids that you minister to week after week know that? How often do you take out the time to really connect with the kids in your ministry? Do you ask Noah how was his weekend and stop to look in his eyes as you wait for a response? Did you tell Jonathan how cool his shoes were, and ask where he got them from? Did you remind Sarah that you know she has a birthday coming up and how amazing it is to turn 7?

We are undoubtedly dealing with digital natives in our ministries, but there will always be traditional ways of connecting that will continue to remain the optimal way. Texting someone to tell them that it is good to see them in church is a good way to touch base, but it is not the same as taking a few minutes to visit with them in person. Sending a happy birthday text is an efficient way to acknowledge them, but stopping by with a card and a piece of birthday cake means so much more.

Now I am the first person to recommend that you utilize technology in your day to day communications, but always **be cognizant that some people need to connect in a more personal way**. For instance, these are the people who prefer handwritten birthday cards in the mail. **Good leaders are sensitive to that and willing go the extra mile when the situation so dictates**. You have to be willing to use a spectrum of engagement that is well- suited to connect with a person's heart and make them feel included, appreciated, and seen. People want to feel apart. Kids want to feel apart. Nobody wants to feel like they are just another number. The same is true for the children in your ministry. Unfortunately, it's easy to get so caught up in our programs that we forget that people want to connect. Consider incorporating the following practices to better connect with the families in your ministry:

- Get to know the needs of the families in your ministry: Do you know the personal needs of the families you serve and the challenges they face? Do you check in on them periodically to personally let them know you are praying for them? If not, it's time to get busy!

- Make eye contact: It's important when communicating with kids or grownups that you not make them feel like a non-factor or nuisance to your productivity. Don't allow your eyes to wander and avoid multitasking with statements like "I'm listening, keep talking."
- Invest in relationships outside of the church: Building relationships with families can be hard if your time with them is limited to Sunday mornings. Be willing to go the extra mile and make plans to meet someone for coffee during the week or be hospitable and invite them over for a meal. Research the afterschool sports and clubs your children are involved in and show up to them from time to time. It's a great way to show them that you really care.

Connecting has a lot of different forms. If all are brought together, you will be considered a connector. In his work, *Everyone Communicates but Few Connect*, John Maxwell reminds us that when it comes to connecting, you want to be better than a good person on a stage. You want to be a person capable of authentically connecting with a child and it not be a show. Just in case you didn't know, kids can read when you're putting on a show, and let me tell you, they're not impressed. A quick way to hinder your chances of a real connection with a child is to be nicer to them when their parents are around than you are to them when they aren't. Kids don't just want a real connection. They need it!

Connection that Brought Forth Transformation

Jesus was the master connector. Jesus' encounter with Zaccheaus was but one of many examples of his incredible ability to connect with people. One of my favorite things about being in Children's Ministry is the opportunity I get to relay these classic Bible stories. While they may be dismissed as "old news" to many adults, KidMin leaders have the privilege of reliving them through the eyes of children. Most of us remember his story through a classic bible song you may have grew up learning when we were little tikes. I can hear the tune in my head right now, "Zaccheaus was a wee little men and a wee little man was he." Like most tax collectors, he didn't have the best reputation among the people. Poor "little" guy, literally. But, in spite of his reputation as a swindler, Jesus wanted to eat at his house. Zaccheaus was shocked that Jesus even noticed him let alone desired to dine at his house. It was clear that Jesus cared more about him than he did about what he did. Others, however, wouldn't have even considered letting him step one foot within their homes without first demanding some evidence of transformation. Jesus wanted to connect, and it was the authentic desire for connection that he displayed to Zaccheaus, which ultimately transformed his life forever.

Wake Up, Get Over Yourself, and Read the Environment

There are a lot of children's ministry leaders who walk into the room so focused on the message that they neglect almost every other element of the service. Unfortunately, their tunnel vision focus on the message eclipses their ability to assess whether the message is in fact connecting. For instance, your preoccupation with leading a worship song with the correct motions may fall flat if the kids refuse to participate. I have seen time and time again leaders do this and the kids remain unmoved. Can you say awkward? The kids are totally disconnected from what is happening on stage, and the leaders have lost yet another opportunity to highlight God's faithfulness.

This means that **effective Children's Ministries moving forward must resolve to abandon the "motions of ministry" in exchange for more effective methods**. At the end of the day, we can't be so consumed with ourselves and our ministries that we misread the environment. A worship leader can tell when the audience is not quite with them. Rather than diving into the next song, they are sensitive to the needs of the people. They get out of who they think they are and attempt to reach the people where they are. Rather than being caught up in the fact that he or she can sing, the worship leader must be in tune with the needs of the broader congregation. Despite challenges in their personal lives, **Children's Ministry Leaders have to develop the skill of being able to read their environments.** You have to be able to identify what is the greatest need. Those who read the environment know when it's time to get off the stage or move closer because you recognize the children need you to be among them. Those who read the environment recognize that despite being 6'2", it may be necessary to wrinkle your clothes and get down on your knees to better connect with your children during prayer time.

Children's Ministry leaders of tomorrow will be intentional about cultivating the ability to assess and identify what a particular service or environment requires. What we bring as leaders is important, but it's not as important as the most critical need in the room. It means recognizing the overall mood of the room, which may dictate an extra song rather than going directly into the lesson. If you notice that the kids are a bit sluggish, you might have them get up and give a high-five to 5 new friends. The point is to never get so caught up in the lesson that you miss the needs of your little audience. At the end of the day, **strive to be committed to do what you came to do while being simultaneously sensitive to what needs to be done to effectively reach the hearts of every child**.

Heart vs. Fact

There's a little girl I know. She was so precious. I remember coming to Children's Church one Sunday morning. In a rush to get into my classroom, I left my husband in the car. Soon after entering the church, I locked eyes with little Suzy as she was galloping down the hall obviously excited about being in Children's Church that day. After one of our workers caught a glimpse of Suzy running down the hallway, she shouted with an aggressive tone, "No running in the hallway!" Unfortunately, the worker was so adamant about enforcing the rules that she completely missed the fact that it was Suzy's birthday. Beyond that, Suzy had not been to church for the past three weeks because it was a known fact that she had faced a number of life challenges over the past couple of weeks. In my estimation, I thought that the worker was way too hard on this sweet little girl.

Even though it's important to enforce the rules, the worker got so caught up in discipline that she missed an amazing opportunity to make a personal connection with a child who so desperately needed it. I believe we failed Suzy that morning. This beautiful little girl immediately lost the smile you could once see from a mile away. Her joy had turned to shame and a feeling of rejection that was similar to what she experienced in her home environment had reared its ugly head. Discipline is certainly a critical factor to maintain classroom decorum and safety, but it is a poor substitute for making a heart connection with those students who need it most.

Every child is coming to your church to be instructed, but they live in a world where everyone is constantly giving them instruction. **Children today need to hear your heart more than your facts**. Over a running incident, little Suzy was made to feel like she had done something so wrong. I remember scanning the room and seeing the expression on her face during worship. Her countenance had changed and her engagement was at an all-time low. I could read her behavior as she questioned in her mind whether she really wanted to be there anymore. I knew it was time to reaffirm my sweet little friend. I stopped everything that I was doing and in Ms. Esther fashion shouted, "Suzy! It is so good to see you today! I have missed you so much! Now come on up here and give me a great big hug!" Little Suzy came running to her Ms. Esther. I got down on her level and told her, "Sometimes I forget to walk in that silly old hallway because it just revs up in me a need for speed." I then grabbed her hand and we skipped down that same hallway together like the rule breakers we were that day without guilt or shame.

The whole point is, as leaders, we can't get so caught up in telling the kids to SIT DOWN or BE QUIET when they're excited about the game or trying to answer questions. Don't risk killing their spirits because you're so caught up in giving them facts on how they need to be quiet and thereby quenching their fire in your setting. Don't blow out their flame. Don't extinguish their excitement in church and risk killing their ability to be fully present in the house of God. Do you know how many leaders I have met who get so caught up being drill sergeants? They come into the classroom screaming "BE QUIET, STOP MOVING or else!" People who do that are killing the environment. Understandably, children need to be guided in the right direction and to develop an appreciation on appropriate conduct in the house of God, but we have to be more focused on the heart than the rule. The teacher who becomes overly concerned with the rule of the room will miss the fact that the kids are excited over Jesus! That's what we want! Don't get so caught up in being the disciplinarian that you miss the precious moment of kids being kids.

As Children's Ministry Leaders, our eyes should forever be on the heart of the matter. The quicker we get to the heart, the more open children will be to the facts. So what type of leader are you? Do you know how to identify with the heart or are you the king or queen of facts? The fact of the matter is that you're trying to teach a lesson, but the heart of the matter is that the children are hungry. The fact of the matter is that you came to preach a word to a group of children, but the heart of the matter is that there is a broken child in your midst whose family just got evicted. They really don't need another flat message but prayer and a reminder that everything is going to be alright. The truth is that you just came to assist in the classroom, but the heart of the matter is that there are kids who are struggling at home and school; and, therefore what God is really calling you to do that Sunday is to be more than an assistant but a beacon of hope and light for his Glory. It's time to stop hitting the snooze button and wake up to matters of the heart!

Key Points

- When you're teaching kids, if they don't feel the connection of your heart in the ministry you're providing, then you're simply doing a production and a production doesn't change lives. Ministry does.
- In order to connect, we must get our ministry to a place where we know who we are ministering to.
- Effective Children's Ministry leaders moving forward must show that they are about more than just a service, but rather about the people in the service.
- Be cognizant that some people need to connect in a more personal way. Good leaders are sensitive to that and willing go the extra mile when the situation so dictates.
- Connecting has a lot of different forms. If all are brought together, you will be considered a connector.
- Effective Children's Ministries moving forward must resolve to abandon the "motions of ministry" in exchange for more effective methods.
- Children's Ministry Leaders have to develop the skill of being able to read their environments.
- Strive to be committed to do what you came to do while being simultaneously sensitive to what needs to be done to effectively reach the hearts of every child.
- Don't get so caught up in being the disciplinarian that you miss the precious moment of kids being kids.
- As Children's Ministry Leaders, our eyes should forever be on the heart of the matter. The quicker we get to the heart, the more open children will be to the facts.

5

The Outside will be more Important than the Inside

"Rise and Shine! Wake Up and remember that People are more important than buildings"

"Go ye therefore, and teach all nations, baptizing them in the name of the Father, and of the Son, and of the Holy Ghost" -Matthew 28:19

Church Building History

100 years ago, the church was a central place for communities, towns, or villages. Prior to that, church was not so centered on a particular building or facility. It was more about intimate interaction between a group of people and their creator. Fast forward, with the evolution of communities, societies, and countries at large, faith continued to grow throughout the nations of the world. Toward that end, church buildings became pillars within the communities. Over time, these cathedrals and sanctuaries became highly revered places of worship and solitude. They were labeled as the place where God presides such that the facility itself became more and more important to the community. Even today, pastors and church leadership have come to pride themselves on the

beauty and size of a sustained structure. However, if you look at church history, the importance was never intended to be so bound around a physical building. The cathedral was an important structure within a community, but in God's eyes the focus was not supposed to be on the building but rather the people inhabiting the building. The greatest example of the original intention of the church can be found in chapter 4 of the book of Acts:

> *All the believers were united in heart and mind. And they felt that what they owned was not their own, so they shared everything they had. The apostles testified powerfully to the resurrection of the Lord Jesus, and God's great blessing was upon them all. There were no needy people among them, because those who owned land or houses would sell them and bring the money to the apostles to give to those in need.*
>
> -Acts 4:32-35

At the start of Christ's church, it was all about people! There was no room for people to care about a facility because it was simply all about the people. People would go house to house and gather in the homes of one another. In fact, if people did own some type of building, it was more common for them to sell it for the purposes of giving money to the needy among them. Ironically, it seems as if today's church has adopted the opposite model. People will regularly come and go, but it's the church building that remains. This "people come and people go" mentality evidences a shift in how we have come to view people in the church. People, or more specifically their resources, are far too often seen as a means to acquiring bigger and better budgets or facilities.

Jesus never built a building. Jesus invested in people. Buildings don't last. They decay and fall apart. If you travel to different parts of the world, you will see a variety of buildings that used to be churches, but have since been converted into hotels, restaurants, or even bars. Just recently I had an opportunity to tour a church turned beautiful bed & breakfast whose owners decided to preserve the original stained glass windows. These gorgeous windows were some of the last remnants of the beautiful church building that once stood there. Many church buildings today are being overtaken by charter schools and other outside programming because the facility is no longer able to sustain itself with the contributions of church members alone. While others are completely losing their facilities all together. **There is no question that the church's value, influence, and place as a central societal bedrock has diminished.** In some measure, this may be a result of our own misplaced priorities, which have elevated the building over the people.

When it comes to Children's Ministry, it is important for us to understand that having that playground, children's wing, state-of-the-art stage, check-in system, or digitally enhanced spaces are great, but it will never matter as much as one soul. **Children matter more than the children's facility**. While a lot of ministry leaders would agree with that statement, there actions do not reflect that truth. Churches that plan to withstand the test of time must understand that their facilities are merely a tool to reach children. Thriving churches of the future will be those that have replaced their facility-focus with a people- focus. Believe it or not, there are a lot of churches who are thriving today despite holding services in rented spaces like schools, hotels, or theaters.

For Children's Ministry leaders across the world, it is a delight and wonder to be able to have a facility where kids can be in awe with all the church has chosen to provide them in the ministry space. But we can't allow the value of ministry to be judged by the space where kids gather rather than the kids who gather in the space. Make your children's ministry children-centered. Your heart is to reach kids and the facility is only one tool of many we use to connect with children. We have to remember the building is only a tool. It's not the church. It's the individuals who represent the church. The building can be demolished and a children's ministry facility can be destroyed. It is only a tool. The nursery is but a tool to nurture children at their most delicate stage of life. Preschool and elementary age spaces are but creative tools to translate the message of hope to children in a way they can understand. To disregard this principle, you will find yourself with a nice space with little to no children. Eventually you will find yourself with no kids and no space because a church with no children is a dying church. And **a church that places a greater premium on its space instead of reaching the families that inhabit the space are the last of a dying breed**.

Make no mistake, there are churches all across America who have invested thousands of dollars into their Kidmin areas with absolutely no return. Some churches have even filed for bankruptcy because of misdirected or ill-timed investments in their physical structures. Most of these churches learned the hard way that if you have a great facility, but terrible individuals working with the kids, no amount of money or investment in a space will keep them coming back. If you don't have a heart-centered ministry whose connection with children exceeds that of the local schools, community centers, Chuck E. Cheese's and Disney Lands of the world, then there will be no competition and you will not be able to sustain. An effective Children's Ministry has to be built up with Christ centeredness in its walls. When we bring kids together, we have to give them something far beyond a cool facility. **Remember, the facility is good, but the presence of God is greater**!

Children's Ministry Facilities Today

Churches today have taken their children's ministry facilities to new heights. You can see Children's Ministry spaces spotlighted in magazines for the marvelous creativity their spaces display. I love visiting churches and touring their facilities. I have never seen two that are quite the same. I am especially impressed by how some churches are able to weave in details that are unique to the children of a particular area. For example, living in Huntsville, Alabama, which is known as "Rocket City," I am so impressed how every Sunday morning our Children's Ministry launches a big rocket in the center of the stage to start the service. There has yet to be a Sunday where I have grown bored with the NASA-like smoke, camera, and countdown.

Years ago it was all about the arch and the steeple. At some point it became all about the details in the stained glass windows and the detailed woodwork of the pews. The more ornate the organ, the better. These were the details that defined the beauty of the space. Today, you can find some Children's Ministry spaces that are competing with Disney World. These Children's Ministry facilities represent significant financial investments and creative designs. They have the right size rooms for the children with state of the art technology built into the room. Their age groups are color coded with special themes for each area. It is a delight to see such advancements because we can finally say after all these years that there is a special space specifically designed and designated for children. The thriving church of tomorrow will have an allocation in the budget designated for the children's ministry, which would ideally include staff to operate the department. The budget will also include an allocation dedicated to curriculum created to reach the heart of today's child. Beyond this, there should be some level of funding for the Children's Ministry teams to periodically attend conferences or conventions to ensure that the leaders grow and develop in the art of reaching children. This will no longer be optional but will be a non-negotiable for the thriving church. But above all of this, we must be certain that all of our Children's Ministry planning, training, and building is inspired by the life-giving Spirit of God. The Bible reminds us of this truth in the book of 2 Corinthians:

> *My message and my preaching were not with wise and persuasive words, but with a demonstration of the Spirit's power, so that your faith might not rest on human wisdom, but on God's power. -2 Corinthians 2:5*

At the end of the day, you can have the best screens and go to the best conferences. You can make the Children's Ministry facility one of the best facilities in the city. You can have excellent workers and color-coded areas. But, without the spirit of God, your Children's Ministry would have missed the heartbeat of God because the goal is not just to be current with emerging trends, but to make sure there's a heart connection between the Father and the child. We should always make sure the service we are giving is equal to that which Jesus gave when he was here on earth. Nice facilities are great but it can't come second to the main thing. **Children's Ministries today that are present without the presence of God will not be present in the future.**

Where Did We Go Wrong

The Bible says we walk by faith and not by sight. So where did we go wrong? We started walking by sight. We started paying more attention to what we saw with our eyes rather than what we were led by in our spirit. As noted in the book of Romans 8:14, "For those who are led by the Spirit of God are the children of God." The Spirit is there to guide us in the way that we should go. The challenge with Children's Ministry is that it can be very program centered. Children's Ministries of the future have to amount to more than just programing. Programs can be rigid. Programs are templates that are set. Unfortunately, a lot of Children's Ministry workers and leaders fall into the trap of being so overly dependent on their curriculum that they miss the move of the Spirit. Instead of being sensitive to God's leading they blindly cling to the agenda or curriculum guideline. The training is important and the curriculum is good, but if God doesn't breathe on it, we will be making mistakes far beyond our wildest imaginations. You cannot do ministry without God centeredness being the guide to operate your ministry.

Where did we go wrong? We were quick to grab the curriculum but we were not quick to pray over the curriculum or invite the Holy Spirit to breathe life and make the curriculum come alive. Where did we go wrong? We became more focused on the seconds, minutes, and hours we had to spend with the children rather than the seconds, minutes, and hours that God has to get a hold of their precious little hearts and minds. One of the goals of ministry is to never become so template-driven that we're not sensitive to what the Holy Spirit is saying. We walk by faith to believe that every child can be touched by Christ, instead of by sight where we can so easily dismiss difficult children as lost.

When you walk by faith, you believe all things are possible. When you walk by sight, you start viewing children as the world does, which may assume that this generation is lost. Leaders who believe that this generation is a lost cause may be serving, but they certainly won't be ministering. Such leaders are only going through the motions of ministry with the children. They may be spending time or conducting a service, but they will not be wholeheartedly fulfilling the Great Commission. The danger with such an approach is that these kids grow up associating with the church, but their true connection is limited to agendas and programs. While all these tools aid the leaders and volunteers, churches must ultimately be place where – as the Word says – Christ be lifted up so that he can draw all men unto himself. In other words, make the curriculum a secondary thing to the main thing.

Make your events and activities second to the main thing. If we're being guided by the Holy Spirit in our ministries, then we can never go wrong. Don't limit your reliance on the Holy Spirit to the selection of a curriculum but invite Him to breathe life on the delivery of it for the kids in your ministry. The curriculum doesn't change lives. It's the Spirit of God that does. Remember, the template should not be exclusively relied upon. The template may be a song with the words. The songs with the words is a guide. The true worship is captured when the person in the front is so sensitive to God's Spirit that they usher the children into the presence of God. The curriculum lesson is the guidebook but it's the minister or teacher that must bring the lesson to life. Self-check-in stations are nice, but it's the greeter that makes the heart connection when they high-five a timid child to let them know they are so glad they are there today. A computer system cannot do that. We can't allow the tools and technology offerings to replace human connections. **The Holy Spirit brings life to a department, not systems. Systems are necessary for an efficient and optimal Children's Ministry, but the Holy Spirit is absolutely essential and must be at the heart of it all.** If you have lost sight of that, it is time to Wake Up!

Paradigm Shift

Everything's changing and the way we originally saw Children's Ministry can no longer be the way we do Children's Ministry. Unfortunately, this is easier said than done because we tend to be creatures of habit. As a church, the older we get the more accustomed we become. At the end of the day, if we are going to reach children in 2020, 2030, and 2040, we have to constantly evaluate the way we do things. Where we understand that planning is critical for success, but we invite the Holy Spirit to breathe on our plans so that we always remain sensitive to His leading. **Our dependence on God ought to be so central that we readily adjust that plan to bring forth ministry**. In other words, the churches of tomorrow will be those with God-led KidMin leaders who incorporate His will into all of their structure, training, and technological components.

This is the paradigm shift. Many Children's Ministries are marked by continued: (1) growth in the number of children and families who attend; (2) periodic training to enhance the effectiveness of their volunteers, and (3) investment into the maintenance and enhancement of their facilities. Yet despite these earmarks of growth, many are still struggling with the challenge of truly strengthening the spiritual maturity of their congregation. These needs will never be addressed if we are missing the main thing. The main thing will always be a God-centered and Spirit-led approach. This shift needs to occur if we are going to move Children's Ministry Forward. If you spend 3 days at a Children's Ministry Conference, you will need to come back and spend 3 days in prayer as to how you will implement these lessons at your church. The time that we spend at our churches need to be more than just decorating rooms and preparing bulletin boards. Don't forget that we're trying to get the presence of God to show up in our lives and in the lives of the precious little flocks. If the facility is great, the curriculum is right, the training has been executed, and the budget has been approved, but there is no presence of God we have still failed. Stated differently, "Unless the Lord builds the house, the builders labor in vain." (Psalm 127:1). If the presence of God does not preside with us, all that we're doing is in vain.

This paradigm shift does not require that we reject planning or strategy, but infuse them with a "with God all things are possible" perspective. It mandates that we return to our first love, Biblical roots, and arrive at the place where everyone was in one accord and the Spirit of God came and rested on them. The goal of Children's Ministry moving forward is to ensure that we allow the supernatural to strengthen every facet of our ministries, irrespective of whether we are in a storefront church or a state of the art facility. This is what allows the coming generation to appreciate that which is eternal. Our God is the same yesterday, today, and forevermore. Remember, we don't want to dismiss the current trends. What we do want to do is bring Christ and those things together so that the next generation will know to be Christian isn't old fashioned. To be Christian isn't to be outdated. **The goal is to bring forth a paradigm shift where trends and faith collide to ensure that nothing is missing in our ministry to children**. When you shift your Children's Ministry approach to the sensitivity of the Holy Spirit, you will be able to better identify when a worker is about to be burned out. You will be able to identify when a child needs special prayer. You will be able to identify when it's time to stop praying and go into a song. You will be able to identify when you need to stop teaching and go into a quiet time. But such a shift requires that we remain sensitive to what God is wanting to do in the midst of all we're doing. This is the paradigm shift.

The Numbers Don't Lie

As we position ourselves to minister to tomorrow's children, it's important for us to understand the numbers. Modern enterprises regularly assess the health and success of their operations through key metrics and measures. The church is no exception. You have to know your numbers. So, the question to you today as the reader of this book is, how many children can your facility accommodate? How many children are there within your community? How many children are there in your zip code? How many children would you like to reach over the next year? How many children have come through your doors in the last 3 months? How many first time visitors have come into your church? As good stewards of what God has entrusted to us, we should be aware of what it costs to open the doors of our churches. **When it comes to serving children, you want to know your numbers. The numbers don't lie**. If your space was built to accommodate 300 children and you are only reaching 80 kids, then you are wasting money and eventually that's going to become a problem. If it doesn't cost you your church, it may cost you your job.

It's important for you to know the numbers as it relates to you and your vision. In other words, how many children does your leadership expect for you to reach on a weekly basis? How much does it cost you to accommodate that many children in the space you are managing? Successful Children's Ministries leverage data to assess the health of their ministries and track their progress toward those measures for the benefit of the children living in their communities. It is a sad day for the Children's Ministry that realizes they have a space that can accommodate 300, but they're only reaching 100 kids every Sunday, in a city that has 200,000 kids where most of them aren't affiliated with any church. It's when you start to gain an understanding of your numbers, you gain a more realistic perspective on how effective you truly are vs. how effective you think you are. In short, **if there are more children on the street than there are in your classroom, then you're doing something wrong**.

As the leader, it's important for you to know the capacity of your ministry and to share that with others. Only aloof Children's Ministry leaders are ignorant to their numbers and disconnected from the capacity of their facilities. These immature leaders are delaying us from making significant strides in the advancement of the faith. Children's Ministry leaders moving forward need to be able to ask the hard questions of whether they are truly impacting the broader community of children and families. If the answer is no, then the effective Children's Ministry will not rest until more children and families are reached. The soccer fields are full. You have to make an appointment to have a party at Chuck E. Cheese. You will wait for over 2 hours to ride a rollercoaster at an amusement park. More children are on a single ride in Disney World than occupy most Children's Churches across the country. The time to Wake Up is now! We have to ask ourselves: why. Now, you don't have to be Disney or Chuck E. Cheese, but you do have to ask yourself what is our competitive advantage. What is it that God has blessed us with that will attract the kids that He has called for us to reach? How can we meet the needs of the children in our spheres of influence? **Know that God has not given you anything that He doesn't intend for you to grow and cultivate.** If he gave you a facility that can hold over 500 children, then you and your team has to believe, without the shadow of a doubt, that you are capable of meeting that threshold. But your vision needs to be clear, and you must consider what it will take to meet the demands of your vision.

There are churches that have grown to multi-site locations because they have a keen understanding of how to reach children and their families. Churches have expanded to two services simply because the Children's Ministry outgrew its space. Every Sunday, how many kids should be in your classroom? What do you need to do as a team to ensure you're meeting those numbers? Why are you down three Sundays in a row? What's happening in your city? What's happening in the lives of your kids? What's happening in your Children's Ministry classrooms that are causing the kids to avoid you? You have to know why the numbers are increasing or decreasing. For a paid ministry person, this is in large part why you are there. You are the one responsible for understanding the management and leadership necessary to take the department to the next phase. Don't get so caught up in photocopying papers and cleaning out supply closets that you miss the boat on leading. Don't get so caught up in distributing handouts at the door and stirring Kool-Aid that you miss implementing the necessary management skills to build healthy teams. Know your role and its great value. There is more we can do! Wake Up!Start by knowing your numbers!

Key Points

- There is no question that the church's value, influence, and place as a central societal bedrock has diminished.
- At the start of Christ's church, it was all about people!
- Children matter more than the children's facility.
- A church that places a greater premium on its space instead of reaching the families that inhabit the space are the last of a dying breed.
- Remember, the facility is good, but the presence of God is greater! Children's Ministries today that are present without the presence of God will not be present in the future.
- The Holy Spirit brings life to a department, not systems. Systems are necessary for an efficient and optimal Children's Ministry, but the Holy Spirit is absolutely essential and must be at the heart of it all.
- Our dependence on God ought to be so central that we readily adjust that plan to bring forth ministry.
- The goal is to bring forth a paradigm shift where trends and faith collide to ensure that nothing is missing in our ministry to children.
- When it comes to serving children, you want to know your numbers. The numbers don't lie. If there are more children on the street than there are in your classroom, then you're doing something wrong.
- Know that God has not given you anything that He doesn't intend for you to grow and cultivate. Put in the work and believe him for the increase

6

Succession

"Sound the alarm! Succession without a Successor is a Failure"

What is Leadership

Leadership is influence. Unfortunately, there are some people in Children's Ministry who believe it's all about the title. Leadership at its lowest level is title-centered. For example, I am the coordinator, I am the director, the pastor just made me the facilitator over this children's group in the Children's Ministry. The list goes on. It is a mistake for people to think that a title alone makes them a leader. Leadership is and will always be influence. Nothing more, nothing less. The inability to lead is a big, big problem in Children's Ministry. This is because most people are attracted to the title of leadership without the understanding of how to lead. **Leadership is all about influencing the area that you are over. If you are not influencing that area, then you are not a leader.** To effectively run a Children's Ministry department, you have to be a leader who leads by influence.

There is a critical need for leaders who can effectively influence their respective areas, irrespective of whether your title reflects it or not. For example, you may be responsible for the check-in station. But if you are incapable of providing guidance to the parents or utilizing the equipment properly, then your leadership over that activity should be reevaluated. If the family pastor has to regularly come to the rescue to bring order or provide guidance, then you are neither adding value nor demonstrating true leadership. The title may be intact, but you're obviously not leading that area in the way that it should be lead. Effective churches of tomorrow require someone who possesses real leadership abilities that can bring direction and order to their prospective areas. A person who cannot bring direction cannot effectively give direction or bring order to an area.

Leadership is also establishing a vision of where you want the ministry to go. When you are a leader you have the ability to see where the ministry is and where it is going. There are a lot of Children's Ministry leaders who have no clue on where they are taking the department. There are others still trying to figure out if they even like children. They may have a commitment to serve, but their leadership qualities have never been fully developed. These leaders are extremely challenged because they don't understand the true definition of leadership.

Leadership requires that you produce results in your area of responsibility. If you cannot produce results, then maybe you're not a leader. No one should ever be chosen to be a leader over a department based solely off of their availability or tenure at the church. Unfortunately, being a long time member is not what makes you a leader. Being a good tither doesn't automatically make you a leader. Even liking kids does not make you a good leader. Now don't get me wrong, all of those things are great qualities to have. Being a long time member at a church, a faithful tither, and one who enjoys children may make you qualified to serve in those respective areas, but it does not qualify you to lead those areas. Children's Ministry leaders of tomorrow must discover what real leadership is, and commit to applying the necessary principles to become a leader. Then and only then will you find yourself producing results.

You cannot depend on your pastor's influence to lead your department. You cannot depend on the student ministry director to lead your department. You cannot depend on the family ministry director to lead your department. Everyone, not just the official ministry staff, can exercise leadership. Even if your area of responsibility is limited to a class with 5 toddlers, you are responsible for studying what it means to grow and develop as an effective teacher. Remember, title is the lowest level when it comes to leadership. But influence breathes life onto the title, which makes you an exceptional person with a title. Always aim for the influence beyond riding the title. If you have to constantly throw out your title, then you are probably struggling to meet other elements of effective leadership. Leadership doesn't just talk the talk, but it must also walk the walk.

A Need for Dynamic Leaders in Children's Ministry

There is a critical need for dynamic leaders in Children's Ministry. **The success of a Children's Ministry rises and falls with the leader.** The need for critical thinking, vision casting, team building, and strategic planning all begins with leadership. The challenge we have in Children's Ministry is that there are a lot of people who have a love for children, but have very little understanding on real leadership. Not only do we need Children's Ministry leaders who are committed to learning how leadership works, but we need leaders who are committed to becoming dynamic in that area of ministry. This is true in all facets of ministry. Leadership is the difference maker when it comes to massive success. Weak leaders produce weak teams, which in turn produce weak departments. If you want to have massive success in Children's Ministry, then the goal should be to become a dynamic leader. Everything about you needs to meet the demand of the calling that God has placed on your life. Leaders are not born, they are developed. Leaders are built. Leaders are called to fulfill an assignment in a particular time, season, or place.

It is important for us to understand that not everyone can lead unless they have developed an ability to lead. Everyone can become a leader, and everyone can become dynamic in their area of leadership if they commit themselves. If our communities, cities, and nations are going to be reached when it comes to next generation ministry 2030 and beyond, there is going to be a massive need for the rising up of men and women dedicated to next level leadership. You can love kids and be a terrible leader. You can love ministry and be a terrible leader. You can be called to ministry and be a terrible leader. You can have a love for your church, a love for God, and be an incredible worshipper, but still be a terrible leader.

Leadership requires cultivation in a person's life. In some people, leadership development takes root at a very early age, but for others they aren't captured until much later in life. For others still, it requires their professional careers or other school experiences that force them to develop leadership skills to meet the demands of the assignment. And this is how dynamic leaders are ultimately born. They decide to meet the demands of the assignment. In other words, we should always be on the lookout for challenges that help to develop our dynamic leadership skills. A dynamic leader consists of certain characteristics:

- **Continual learners:** leaders are continual learners. Leaders are readers. Leaders are engaged in becoming better in the areas assigned to them.
- **Focus on vision:** Leaders focus on vision not things. Things come and go but vision is the ultimate reason why leaders exist. A leader has the ability to see beyond where they are to where they are going. A leader without a vision is not a leader at all, but simply someone with a title.
- **People-centered over program-centered:** If you don't have a team, you're not a leader. If people are not following you, you are not a leader. In Children's Ministry, we need leaders who understand that they need people in order to fulfill their assignment. Jesus said to his disciples "Follow Me, and I will make you fishers of men." (Matthew 4:19 NKJV). Even Jesus understood that in order to fulfill his assignment in the earth he needed people. The greater your assignment the more people you're going to need. The greater the magnitude of your Children's Ministry, the more people skills you will have to develop. Dynamic leaders understand that it's not their charisma on the stage, or their

academic accolades, or who they know. It's all about who they can bring and build around them for a common goal to advance the kingdom. Dynamic leaders are what Children's Ministry needs and will continue to need well into the future. Unless you become the leader that is capable of meeting the demand of the vision that has been placed on your Children's Ministry, then your department will be limited in what it is able to produce. It is time to Wake Up and become a dynamic leader and influence your church and community for God.

Building a Healthy Team

When a true leader emerges, a group of people are always there to connect with that leader to support him or her to meet the demands of their leadership. When Jesus came on the scene after being baptized, He came out of the water and the Father said "This is My beloved Son, in whom I am well pleased." (Matthew 3:17 NKJV). After Jesus' identity was confirmed and His leadership affirmed, it was then that he started to call the disciples. Whenever God calls a leader, he calls a group of people to assist that leader in fulfilling his or her assignment. A great leader is made even greater by those who surround them. In Children's Ministry, you need leaders with vision but you also need leaders with dynamic people around them.

Leadership is going to be gauged hugely on the leader's ability to build a team. Teams don't automatically come together, people build them. Teams are formed, teams are developed, and teams are built from the ground up. It takes time to build a healthy team. You could be called to lead and have weighty vision, but if you are not surrounded by the right support structure, then you will become a frustrated leader. So, if you are going to do incredible things for the Kingdom through your Children's Ministry, then you need to first gain a healthy perspective on how to build a healthy team. Building a healthy team is critical for next level ministry. Here are some characteristics of a team that is being cultivated correctly:

- **Different people:** A team composed of a complete homogenous group – same thinking, background, experience, and opinions – will be a weaker team. A healthy team has different people who encompass a variety of skills and experiences, which if properly harnessed will truly enrich every facet of Children's Ministry. You don't want all militant people. You don't want all funny people. You don't want all creative people. You don't want all intellectual people. What you need is a little bit of everybody! The challenge is that we typically attract people who are very similar to us. So whoever the leader is, that's the type of people that they normally attract. In order to avoid a "carbon-copy team," you have to be very intentional in recruiting people with different personalities and strengths. In short, try to identify more of what you need vs. more of who you are when building a healthy team.
- **Teaching people to work well together:** Bringing people together is one thing, but teaching them how to work together is a completely different skill set. There are a lot of wonderful teams that fail because of their inability to work well together. This is where the leader adds value. It is the leader's responsibility to bring these people together by focusing them on a common goal. There is incredible power that comes from a team that is on one accord. A team who puts their differences aside and embraces each individual's distinct differences is a team that will go far! At the end of the day, differences are necessary for healthy teams to perform at their best. When building a team, personalities can clash and jealousy can arise, but it takes a skilled leader to bring all of those differences together.
- **You have to be able to correct and inspire:** When a leader is unable to correct, challenge, and inspire their team, they will never be able to reach their highest potential. You know you have a weak team if the members are unwilling to receive constructive feedback. A leader who cannot challenge or inspire their team will never take the Children's Ministry department

to the place that it's capable of going. Such skill can only be developed through the building of relationships.

- **Authentic appreciation for people:** In order to build a healthy team, one must be able to appreciate people for who they are and not just for what they bring. You have to be able to identify that people are valuable beyond their gifts. So if you want to build a healthy team, let your team members know that you care more about them (and not just their volunteer service). People want to be loved, cared for, and appreciated. When a person has committed to joining you in your assignment to reach the next generation, you want to let them know that they matter beyond their ability to serve children. Does your team know that you care about them?

No One Is Forever

Everyone is going to be replaced. Everyone has a timeline during which their service will come to an end. It doesn't matter who you are or how good you are at something, all good things must come to an end. There will always be a timeline on a leader's ability to serve. The truth of the matter is that no one is forever, and in order for us to have a sustainable ministry we should study Jesus and his model.

The first thing Jesus did was to identify His call, and what He came to the earth to accomplish. The second thing that He did was to identify who was called to help Him to fulfill His mission and carry forward the mission thereafter. If your ministry only survives and thrive while you are leading it, then your service would have not been a success. Success without a successor is failure. Jesus gave us the recipe for sustainable success in our ministries. Yes, God has called us to be the best leaders that we can be while we are leading. However, successful Children's Ministry leaders lead with the mindset that tomorrow it will be necessary to train others to be able to sustain the ministry. **Every leader should build the ministry in such a way to ensure that it can thrive in their absence.**

When it comes to leadership, there is a misperception that if the ministry excels after we leave, then that means we were a failure. This misperception can cause us to be ashamed if we discover that the ministry has doubled in size after our retirement. However, I truly believe that every leader has an appointed time and season of ministry during which they serve. **You must serve your time and then have the courage to pass the baton.** The goal is to give the best service in your time and lay such an incredible foundation that your successor can launch to even higher heights. If you leave and the ministry does well, then be grateful because you have set the stage for them to do well. We have to stop questioning our service when those who come after us do well. Most leaders are able to perform well because of the bricks that were laid by the leader that came before them. At the end of the day, there is nothing to celebrate if a ministry crumbles in your absence. Similarly, new leadership should not boast or act as if the prior leadership made no contribution to their current successes. It is nothing to celebrate when you depart from a ministry position and the department goes downhill. Such reactions are actually a reflection of weak leadership ill-equipped to effectively transition governance of the ministry. The proper way to build a healthy department is not to celebrate that the numbers were up while you were there, but rather that the numbers continue to go up after you're gone. **Strong Children's Ministries of the future will build with transition in mind**.

Building a Healthy Culture of Transition

Transition is necessary for healthy growth in ministry. Anyone wanting to stay in a ministry forever will ultimately become a problem for that ministry. No one is forever. In order for a ministry to thrive, there has to be an understanding that people will come and people will go. **Attrition in a ministry is not necessarily an indicator of poor health. All release is not bad release. Release is necessary for health**. During the course of a tree's life, it must lose leaves in order to grow. If the body only takes in and never releases, then the body will become sick. Children's Ministry is no exception. People are going to come and people are going to go because it is necessary for them to transition.

People transition for many different reasons. The problem is that we don't like how it feels when people leave so we may unknowingly get in the way of God's assignment. We have to start teaching that there are three types of people who show up in our ministry. There are people who are there for a reason. There are people who are there for a season. There are people who are prepared to be there for a lifetime. People who are there for a reason may have heard about a special event and they want to help kick it off. People who are there for a season may have just moved into the city for a stint. They are looking to attend and serve at a church locally and have chosen yours, but that season will end when they have to move again. Finally, there are those who seem as if they are prepared to serve in our ministries for a lifetime. They will commit to serve the ministry for as long as it takes. This is why Children's Ministries moving forward should build a culture that recognizes that no one is forever.

Everyone is ultimately going to transition. No matter how much you love the children's pastor of today, they will not be the children's pastor of tomorrow. The children's worship leader of today, will not be the children's worship leader of tomorrow. The director of vacation bible school today, will not be the director of vacation bible school tomorrow; and that's okay! Even the disciples had to accept when it was Jesus' time to go. They may not have liked it, but Jesus made it clear that the transition was necessary:

> *Nevertheless I tell the truth. It is to your advantage that I go away; for if I do not go away, the Helper will not come to you; but if I depart, I will send Him to you. John 16:7 (NIV)*

Jesus had to eventually go away so that the helper could come. Who is the Helper? The Holy Spirit who took Jesus' ministry forward upon his ascension. Who is your helper? The next person who is going to come and take your ministry to the next level. Someone is going to replace all of us. **If I stay where I don't belong because I want to be present forever, I will hurt the very thing that I intended to bless.** If I want to be a blessing, then I need to serve faithfully while I'm present and transition at the appropriate time. If I overstay my appropriate time, then I hinder the next person. Jesus said he had to go, because one is coming who will be able to empower you beyond even what he was able to do. He is called the Holy Spirit, the guide, and the difference maker.

All of us will encounter people who are greater than us. **We have to mature to a point where we accept and welcome our successors**. It's this healthy mindset that appreciates that kingdom ministry is more about the work being performed than the pride one feels about their personal legacies. Our goal should always be that God be lifted up through each part of the body. This means that we should be intentional to involve many different people in ministry. Each one bringing glory to God by running the race set out before them as God has purposed, and knowing when to pass the baton to their successor in due season. It's time to Wake Up and get serious about your succession plan.

Key Points

- ❖ Leadership is all about influencing the area that you are over. If you are not influencing that area, then you are not a leader.
- ❖ Leadership requires that you produce results in your area of responsibility.
- ❖ You cannot depend on your pastor's influence to lead your department.
- ❖ It is important for us to understand that not everyone can lead unless they have developed an ability to lead.
- ❖ Leadership is gauged hugely on one's ability to build a team.
- ❖ Every leader should build the ministry in such a way to ensure that it can thrive in their absence.
- ❖ Everyone is ultimately going to transition. Strong Children's Ministries of the future will build with transition in mind.
- ❖ Attrition in a ministry is not necessarily an indicator of poor health. All release is not bad release. Release is necessary for health.
- ❖ You must serve your time and then have the courage to pass the baton.
- ❖ We have to mature to a point where we accept and welcome our successors.

7

Candid Conversations

"Stop hitting the snooze button! Addressing the critical hard issues of today is critical for success moving forward."

"but, speaking the truth in love, may you grow up in all things into Him who is the head – Christ" -Ephesians 4:15 (NKJV).

Confrontation In Ministry

One sign of a great leader is his or her ability to deal with confrontation. Very few Children's Ministry leaders have taken the time to squarely address challenges. If you lead a thriving and progressive children's ministry for any extended period of time, then you will inevitably have to deal with certain challenging subjects. There are certain events that occur which may cause people to operate in their feelings. When hostile or hurt feelings emerge, then confrontation is in inevitable. People will get personal in ministry when there is no need to get personal. This may be due to their lack of spiritual maturity or inability to understand how ministry functions. You may find yourself addressing certain topics that can become very heated. One thing is for sure, avoiding confrontation will never help you in Children's Ministry today or in the future. The following three things are essential for any leader when dealing with confrontation:

- **They need to be spiritually sensitive:** Failure to be spiritually sensitive will cause you to operate in your feelings. This may cause the other person to respond to you in a negative way. Spiritual sensitivity allows you to identify the appropriate timing and the way something might need to be addressed.
- **Connect with the heart before the issue:** The other person should know and hear that you care, love, and appreciate who they are first before the subject matter that needs to be addressed. They need to be assured that the conversation at hand is not a personal attack, but that you truly love them with the love of the Lord before anyone gets offended.
- **Other mature individual's involvement:** If you are going to confront another person, it's important that you do so with a Biblical approach and perspective. To the extent your individual attempt to address the offensive behavior fails, the agreement and support of other leaders in the department may be necessary. They will provide an unbiased and objective view of the situation you are going to address with the ultimate goal of continued ministry to children and their families. Some instances may require you to bring in others. One on one confrontation has the ability to become very nasty and escalate really fast. It's important that you have others who can attest to the fact that you tried your best to respond to the situation in the healthiest manner, so that when it's all said and done, if others need to be involved in the situation it will be known that you went about it in the most mature manner where Christ was glorified.

What is Considered Taboo

Gender Appropriation with Children

Despite being a taboo topic, **the church must be prepared to address prevailing issues of the day**, including the popular concept of gender fluidity. Children's Ministry leaders are going to have to become very skilled at understanding the best ways to address it. It is possible for you to have an opinion and be wrong. It is possible to have an inappropriate understanding based off of cultural traditions. This is why our responses need to go beyond a binary "this is right" or "this is wrong." For the coming generation, this superficial explanation just isn't enough. To them, growing up in the church doesn't make you right, but rather very opinionated.

It's important that we understand today's children are being challenged to question their very gender. **Children's Ministry Leaders moving forward must study how to appropriately guide children in the way that they should go without sounding like an uneducated person.** You may feel strongly about your position, but your opinion must be grounded in more than your personal views. When you open your mouth, make sure that you are informed as to what you are saying. Many Children's Ministry leaders are woefully uninformed on prevailing topics of the day, particularly when it comes to emerging concepts in sexual identity and orientation. Many of us have opinions, but limited facts to support our opinions. It's important that we understand that children today may need reinforcement of their true identity, which is buttressed by a Biblical world view. These explanations, however, must not only take place from an eloquent standpoint, but must be rooted in a reasoned, researched, and intellectually solid foundation. They must connect the Biblical dots while simultaneously doing so in a way that opens up the child to understanding the grave importance of this concept.

We can't be afraid to address a subject, but we can't address a subject where we have limited knowledge. It is ignorance at its highest level to get loud about a subject that you know nothing about. **Children's Ministry leaders moving forward need to take the time to study the subjects that are affecting the children in their ministry**. Gender, sexuality, and sexual identity is a subject that is not going anywhere. Get informed to ensure that you can properly present your case if the need arises because you are leading a ministry to children and their families.

For instance, there was a girl that attended a church who despite her biological gender started to identify as a boy. Under the influence of school and popular culture, this little girl had the full support of her parents. This little girl loved her church, but now was at a juncture where she wanted her church to support her truth. Once she made the confession that she needed to go to the boy's bathroom instead of the girls, the church found itself in a challenging situation. Despite being a national issue, the church was ill- prepared to address the situation. How prepared are you?

Sex

Sex is a subject matter worthy of critical attention, but is being ignored by many Youth and Children's Ministries. We live in a sex-saturated world where the subject is so prevalent that many of the kids in our ministries already know all about it. Fewer and fewer children are asking, "where do babies come from?" because they are growing up with the understanding that mommy and daddy came together to make me.

Lack of education and understanding of the role sex plays in our society, and how we should be educating our children in the church is a huge problem. Even if it is mentioned in church circles, it's generally far below the level of communication it needs to be. As much as we hate to admit it, we have little boys and girls in our Children's Ministries that are exposed to mature subjects that are far beyond their years. Effective Children's Ministry leaders of tomorrow will not be afraid to address the challenging subjects. A little girl mentioned the word sex in Sunday school and the teacher responded with, "We don't use the 'S' word in here." Such responses in this day and age will only widen the disconnect between us and the next generation. **We have to be willing to discuss difficult concepts and help children understand them from God's perspective.** At some point our children will do more than just talk about sex so we must be prepared to equip them with a Biblical understanding.

Admittedly, the word "sex" is viewed as taboo or off limits until we're 21, 25, or in the case of my kids, 37! But we cannot run from the word sex any longer. The reality is that sex has been around since the beginning of time. But it's no secret that the word has garnered some negative connotations, especially in the church. As next generation leaders we must be honest regarding the topic of sex and guide our children toward Biblical truth. Such explanations will honestly broach the topic in a way that is age appropriate, reinforced in the home, Biblically-grounded, and relevant to today. We should never make children feel ashamed because of their questions. Of course, as the Children's Ministry department, we are not going to be the primary place to speak to what sex is and what sex is not, but we must be one of the voices on the subject. If we are going to counterbalance many of the inaccurate or demonic opinions on the subject, we can't be afraid to point our children to God's opinion on the matter.

A child may come into your ministry space and touch another child inappropriately, albeit in an innocent manner, based off of what they are exposed to in the home. We need to be able to address that in a manner that protects all parties and brings about a healthy understanding. To permanently remove a child and forbid them from returning to children's church is not the appropriate response. Children's Ministry Leaders must learn how to proactively address these issues rather than being reactive. It's time for us to stop putting our heads in the sand and acting like our kids are completely insulated from the sexual suggestive content on TV, school, or online. It's everywhere and we cannot completely avoid it. If we turn a blind eye to them, we become irrelevant and lose our ability to connect with a generation that so desperately needs our guidance. **It is vital that we become more relevant and skilled at addressing the subjects that are confronting our kids and their families**. Here are 5 tips on how to address taboo subject matters:

- We have to have a policy as a church to speak to all relevant subject matter.
- We have to partner with the family ministry department to ensure that we are offering the appropriate parenting seminars, workshops, and roundtables to help educate and highlight to parents the ever changing topics that are affecting children

today. We need parents to lead the way in addressing these subjects.

- We need the senior pastors to address the fact that children are being exposed to explicit content at alarming ages and help lead the effort on the biblical way we are to respond. Also, consider making resources available to children and their families that will help them start the conversation at home in a healthy way. Here are a few suggestions to help you get started:
    - o *God Made Your Body*, by Jim Burns - Recommended Ages: 4-6
    - o *How God Makes Babies*, by Jim Burns- Recommended Ages: 6-9
    - o *God Made All of Me*, by Justin & Lindsay Holcomb -Recommended Ages: 2-8
    - o *Good Pictures, Bad Pictures*, by Kristen Jenson & Gail Poyner - Recommended Ages: 7-12
    - o *A Child's First Book on Marriage*, by Jani Ortlund - Recommended Ages: 4-9
    - o *The Ultimate Girls' Body Book*, by Dr. Walt Larimore & Dr. Amarylis Sanchez Wohliver - Recommended Ages 9-12
    - o *The Princess and The Kiss*, by Jennie Bishop - Recommended Ages: 6-9
    - o *Gender*, by Brian Seagraves & Hunter Leavine -Recommended Ages: Adult
    - o *Mom, Dad...What's Sex?*, by Joel Fitzpatrick & Jessica Thompson - Recommended Ages: Adult

Mental Illness among Young People

Mental illness is become increasingly more important for church leaders to understand. It's no secret that the church needs to play a more aggressive role when it comes to addressing mental health. The truth is that mental illness affects many people, including church members.

As ministers of the gospel, we have to train our volunteers to recognize the difference between mental illness or behavioral disorders and disciplinary issues. In other words, not all behavior is bad behavior but may in fact be tied to mental illness or other diagnosable conditions. Unfortunately, for many Children's Ministry leaders, this is another area where many are uninformed. It can be difficult to recognize whether a child is acting out or struggling from a much deeper issue. The child with Tourette syndrome is not trying to be disruptive, but can have little control over what they say due to a breakdown in their nervous system. Mental illness has always been around. The difference today is that society is becoming more informed. The church has become a haven for people struggling with massive emotional challenges and treating them with the remedy of faith. It is important that we not attack those who are struggling with such challenges, but work alongside them to help them deal with their mental illness in a healthy way. **The church should be a beacon of light that preserves their dignity while encouraging them to get the help that they need**.

It's important to know that people who struggle with mental illness are normal people. These are people who are capable of still performing. They are people who still want to worship God. They are people who still want to be involved. They are people who are passionate about serving and advancing the kingdom. They simply have a challenge that you and I may not have, but they are still capable and valuable in the kingdom of God. When it comes to mental illness, we need to be cognizant that there are people in our midst who are suffering from clinical depression, bipolar disorder, anxiety, post- traumatic stress disorder, among others. People diagnosed with such ailments are not damaged goods and should know that the church is a safe place where they can talk about their challenges without being judged or stigmatized.

Children's Ministry Leaders of tomorrow must stay informed about mental health as it affects both children and the workers that serve in the ministry. The church of tomorrow will need to train their people on how to recognize symptoms of depression, stress, abuse, Oppositional Defiant Disorder (ODD), Tourette Syndrome, Obsessive

Compulsive Disorder (OCD), and other emotional, behavioral, or mental health struggles that commonly affect children. Your readiness in this area could not only impact how we reach them for Christ, but may even save a life. If we are truly going to be the best ambassadors for His kingdom, we need to invest in gaining expertise on the best methods of reaching families who are facing these challenges. At the end of the day, we want to be skilled, informed, and able to help those who call our church home at their various points of need.

Leadership Indiscretions

We can't talk about that. We don't see pastor any more, but we can't talk about that. Effective immediately, we have a new Children's Ministry Director while the prior one and his wife still attend the church, but we can't talk about that. There was a fight in adult church between Elder Phillip and Deacon Andrew, but kids; we can't talk about that either. Leaders make mistakes all the time. When we avoid addressing those mistakes, we alienate young people who are just as aware that something bad has occurred. Unaddressed leadership indiscretions are a major problem in the church of Christ. Time and time again, I have seen situations occur where congregational prayers are solicited, but the indiscretions are swept under the rug. It's important for us to let people know that the pastor, children's director, worship leader, and parents are all fallible and prone to err. We are all human and struggling to live in a sinful world which is governed by demonic forces. Ephesians 6:12 reminds us of this truth:

> *For our struggle is not against flesh and blood, but against the rulers, against the authorities, against the powers of this dark world and against the spiritual forces of evil in the heavenly realms. -Ephesians 6:12 (NIV)*

The truth is that our human nature wrestles with good and bad decisions. Every now and then, the bad has a tendency to prevail. Even in ministry, it is possible for the Children's Ministry Director to make a mistake that may lead to a leadership indiscretion. It is possible for the senior pastor to make a mistake that can become a leadership indiscretion. These leadership indiscretions have the power to break the hearts of children, mess with the minds of the congregation, and disrupt people's faith in God. Even though these indiscretions are to be considered sin, we must remember that we all have sinned and fallen short of the glory of God. In challenging situations like these, it is always best to reflect upon the heart of Jesus. We all can recall the familiar story of the woman caught in the act of adultery. In the gospel of John, Jesus gave us a powerful example to live by when handling indiscretions:

> *When they kept on questioning him, he straightened up and said to them, 'Let any one of you who is without sin be the first to throw a stone at her.' -John 8:7*

Jesus saw the woman, not her sin. He showed grace and encouraged others to do the same while urging her, in love, to sin no more. Our response should be similar. Yes, there will be disappointment and consequences as a result of the leadership indiscretions. Nonetheless, we should build a culture of grace where our people know that we live in a fallen world and our enemy is real. We can't let our kids' faith and the faith of those in our congregation rest upon the unreliable foundation of people's righteousness. At any point, we are susceptible to making bad choices. As leaders, we are to hand such situations over to God and allow him to do what he sees fit while strengthening the body that remains.

Why Are We Afraid to Address the Tough Subjects

Ignorance on the Topic

We just don't know. To make matters worse, we don't want to admit that we just don't know. But ignorance should not be an excuse. Just because we don't know, does not give us license to remain uninformed.

A Children's Ministry leader who thinks they know it all, is not a good Children's Ministry leader. Every one of us will find ourselves in a place where we simply don't have the answer. But we cannot allow the work of Jesus Christ to be limited because of our inability to address a subject. Even when you don't know where to begin, the good news is, there is always someone around who does. Effective Children's Ministry Leaders of the future will know when it's time to bring in the experts. Why? Because we need to know! Maybe that means partnering with the Police Department to learn the best way to respond when it comes to an active shooter. Maybe you need to partner with the hospital to bring someone in to teach your team how to recognize signs of abuse.

I recently had the honor of being a part of the "Influencers Summit," an annual conference designed to train attendees on how to effectively reach the next generation by maximizing their influence. Being held in Nassau, Bahamas, the 2019 Influencers Summit attendees had to be very sensitive to the devastating impact that Hurricane Dorian had across the islands. With over thousands of people being displaced, the leadership determined that it was necessary to address this crisis in a meaningful way. Sensitive to this crisis, the leadership sponsored a workshop geared toward providing solace in times of crisis, and commissioned a team to conduct a service and provide donations for displaced children. This workshop was heavily attended because it was specifically designed to aid those communities to and effectively support those children who may be suffering from extreme trauma following a disruption and devastation of a category 5-hurricane unlike any the island has seen before.

Don't put pressure on yourself to have all of the answers. Someone else knows what you don't and is willing to help you. Too many Children's Ministry leaders hurt their departments because they don't want to admit that they just don't have all of the answers. You're more of an impressive leader when you are sober-minded enough to know and admit your strengths and deficiencies. Those leaders know when to seek support to enhance their ministries. **Leaders must get the help that they need because willful ignorance is never an excusc and will cause you to fail your Children's Ministry department**.

Fear of Overexposing Young People

Too often in Children's Ministry we avoid critical conversation topics as a result of fear of overexposing young people. The reality is that kids know more than we think they know. We must remember that fear is of the devil and, if left unchecked, will cripple you and your department. It is vital that we are honest with our kids because the truth will set you free. If something needs to be addressed, then we have to prepare ourselves to address it. Often times fear comes from our lack of knowledge and our inability to address matters when they need to be addressed. **Effective Children's Ministry Leaders moving forward will not lead from a place of fear, but will have the courage to face the necessary issues head on**. God's instructions to Joshua resonates more clearly on this point:

> *This is my command – be strong and courageous! Do not be afraid or discouraged. For the Lord your God is with you wherever you go. -Joshua 1:9 (NLT)*

You must cancel fear and tell it that it has no place in your life or Children's Ministry. At the end of the day, your job is to raise up healthy spiritual champions. **Boys and girls who will know that we love them so much that we aren't afraid to discuss the difficult subjects**. We want to make sure that they are equipped at the highest level so their faith will remain as they grow older. This is precisely why we must move away from old traditions that have no power in reaching the hearts of this newer generation.

> *"And so you cancel the word of God in order to hand down your own tradition. This is only one example among many others." -Mark 7:13 (NLT)*

Tradition does not move the will of God. As human beings, we are prone to operate in tradition. Traditions take root when a common practice is done over an extended period of time. If you want to be the ministry that is continuously reaching young people in a healthy way, we have to be open to letting go of ineffective traditions. We have to remember that there is a time and a season for everything, including traditions. **Yes, traditions ought to be celebrated and appreciated, but we must never let them drain the vitality out of our departments. Our goal should always be to stay on the pulse of God's desire for a generation**. Jesus himself did not come to embrace tradition but to establish what was needed for that time. As Children's Ministry Leaders moving forward, we must follow his example of honoring the traditions of the past without letting them paralyze you from moving ahead in the future. Stop hitting the snooze button on taboo topics. The future will not give us room to hide our heads in the sand any longer if we are truly going to reach the next generation. May we all Wake Up together as the body of Christ and thus further the kingdom of God for generations to come!

Key Points

- ❖ One sign of a great leader is his or her ability to deal with confrontation.
- ❖ The church must be prepared to address prevailing issues of the day.
- ❖ Children's Ministry leaders moving forward must study how to appropriately guide children in the way that they should go without sounding like an uneducated person.
- ❖ Children's Ministry leaders of tomorrow need to take the time to study the subjects that are affecting the children in their ministry.
- ❖ It is vital that we become more relevant and skilled at addressing the subjects that are confronting our kids and their families.
- ❖ Lack of education and understanding of the role sex plays in our society, and how we should be educating our children in the church is a huge problem.
- ❖ The church should be a beacon of light that preserves the dignity of those living with mental illness while encouraging them to get the help that they need. Children's Ministry Leaders of tomorrow must stay informed about mental health as it affects both children and the workers that serve in the ministry.
- ❖ A Children's Ministry leader who thinks they know it all, is not a good Children's Ministry leader.
- ❖ Leaders must get the help that they need because willful ignorance is never an excuse and will cause you to fail your Children's Ministry department.
- ❖ Effective Children's Ministry Leaders moving forward will not lead from a place of fear, but will have the courage to face the necessary issues head on.

Conclusion

Everything is changing. If we are truly going to reach the generation of tomorrow, it is vital that we embrace this truth. Our success will hinge on our ability to shift our methods as needed. Our inability to communicate with these digital natives in their language can result in dire consequences. We must resist the temptation to wing it and commit to creative teaching methods designed to reach every child. The key to unlocking their hearts to the gospel of hope is when our care for children outweighs our need to be right. We need to take out the time to study the subjects that are affecting our children. The time is now. We have to become serious about how we do Children's Ministry.

Examining our programs and strategies for reaching children is going to be the difference maker if we are going to reach the next generation for Christ. Building strong teams, developing healthy succession plans, and knowing our numbers will be pivotal. Remember, God hasn't given you anything that he doesn't want you to cultivate. Put in the work and believe him for the increase. The generation of tomorrow is depending on it.

I hope this book has blessed you as much as it has blessed me writing it. I would love to hear about it. Drop me a message at childsheart83@gmail.com and let me know what wake up calls you received. You have been appointed for such a time as this. The church is and should always be a beacon of light. Remember, information received and not applied is useless. Together we can reach children if we do it more effectively. It's time to wake up!

HERE'S WHAT PEOPLE HAVE TO SAY ABOUT ESTHER'S NEWEST BOOK.......

Esther Moreno has written a concise battle plan for reaching the next generation for Christ. *Children's Ministry Wake Up Call* offers tangible and practical formulas to shift your method of gospel presentation to a post Christian world. Don't get left behind in the race to reach as many kids as we can for the kingdom. Before going into any battle we must have the right weapons. Esther's book will equip you with the tools you need to make an impact on your community. If you have been doing things the way they have always been done, let this amazing book be your wake up call!

Kevin Adkins – Children's Pastor
Life Church Huntsville
Huntsville, Alabama

This book is a must read for every Children's Ministry leader around the world passionate about effectively reaching the next generation. It is relevant and cutting edge. The country of origin maybe be different, but the challenges faced by this new generation is generally the same. The heart of the author is evident in the book. She encourages us not to just do ministry for service sake. We want to do ministry for the sake of the people we are serving. If we have the children's time and attention, then we should endeavor to make it count. Children's Ministry leaders are encouraged to embrace the digital age and effectively use it in developing new methods to reach this new generation while adhering to unchanging principles. This book encourages boldness, innovation and creativity among members of the children's ministry team. As a children's ministry director in the Bahamas I appreciate the wisdom and insight found in this book. The wisdom gained from reading this book and put to practice will inevitably help move your children's ministry to the next level.

Minister Angela Nixon – Children's Ministry Director
Living Waters Kingdom Ministries
Nassau, Bahamas

I've known Esther Moreno for a while now and we share this unique calling to reach the next generation, which has connected us in so many different ways. From doing conferences together to standing in front of children and traveling together. In this book, the biggest challenge of our lives is dealt with, how are we going to reach out to young people with a Christ centered message in an ever-changing world? She addressed the war on children's lives ahead and how to prepare for it. Every Leader in Children's Ministry should be aware of what is coming ahead of us with respect to reaching young people, which Esther shares in this book. If we do not prepare for this, we stand the risk of watching young people who are coming after us totally consider church an ancient idea.

Naziri Komundage – Founder & CEO
Children Missions International
Kampala, Uganda

As Children's Ministry leaders we are at a crossroads, defined by digital technology. The biggest challenges in reaching the next generation, is not travelling to outlying or remote areas or finding the right curriculum, but it is presenting the gospel in a way that is easy, comfortable and familiar to them. This book is an easy read, filled with timely and relevant information.

It encourages and guides Children's Ministry leaders through the pitfalls faced when technology is not embraced. It encourages Children's Ministry leaders to grasp and embrace the tools that will allow them to present the "message of hope" to the most fruitful audience.

Eunice R. Perpall – National Leader
Child Evangelism Fellowship- Bahamas
Nassau, Bahamas

Esther Moreno implores Children's Ministry leaders to "appreciate changing seasons and to prepare themselves for the coming war." This work is an urgent invitation to "Stop over analyzing and produce." Esther candidly discusses the tough subjects of confrontation in ministry and taboo topics children are facing today. This vibrantly anointed leader addresses hot topics head-on. Esther unashamedly helps the church grasp what must be done now in order to have a thriving children's ministry tomorrow. It starts with you reading this thought-provoking call to action today.

Sherry Chester – Children's Pastor
The Way Bible Church
Sulphur Springs, TX

This book is a must read for all children's ministry leaders and pastors who are serious about reaching the children of this generation. It is packed full of insights and knowledge that will help you to skillfully sharpen your ministry efforts in this era. It's not just coming from the pen, but from the heart of an experienced and youthfully exuberant children's pastor with love and passion. So grab your team and get ready to create an effective, ever evolving ministry equipped for generations to come.

Larriston Gaynor - Director
National Children's Ministry
New Testament Church of God, Jamaica

CPSIA information can be obtained
at www.ICGtesting.com
Printed in the USA
FSHW011325201219
65187FS

9 781796 078060